Golf Smart

7 Secrets
To Master The
Mind Game Of Golf

Dr. Marilyn J. Varcoe

Allan Productions
Phoenix, Arizona

Golf Smart

7 Secrets to Master the Mind Game of Golf

Printed in the United States of America.

Reprinted by permission from:
Appendix A: New Harbinger Publications, Oakland, CA 94609
Appendix B: Dr. Bob Phillips, Norcross, GA

Book publication by Allan Productions, Phoenix, AZ, a division of GS Inc. Cover design by Foster Reznor. Editing by Janina Birtolo. Cover photo at Bay Colony Golf Club by Tim Stamm. Inside photography provided courtesy of Rick Sharp. 1999 Ryder Cup shirt compliments of Chuck Copley of the Jeffrey Rose Corporation and John Bevevino, Preston Piermattei and Ben Crenshaw. Text design by Ad Graphics, Inc. Illustrations by Illustration Alley, Inc. Venturi photos courtesy of Ken Venturi. Sarazen photos courtesy of Mary Ann Sarazen.

Library of Congress Catalog Number: 94-012045

ISBN: 0-9676670-0-3

Attention Corporations

Copies of this book are available at special quantity discounts for bulk purchases, sales, promotions, education or fund raising. Contact: Golf Smart, Inc., PO Box 770412, Naples, FL 34107-0412. Phone: (941) 514-3015, (888) 404-9682, Fax: (941) 514-7822, or Allan Productions, PO Box 51102, Phoenix, AZ 85076. Website: http://www.golfsmart.net or E-mail: drvarcoe@golfsmart.net.

What others are saying about
Golf Smart

"I really enjoyed reading this book. Marilyn Varcoe well understands how to master the mind game of golf. Her experience as a golf psychologist has allowed her to see what works. Her tips on relaxation, mental strength, confidence and fostering a positive attitude can help you play in your head as much as on the course."

– Ken Venturi
CBS Sportscaster & former PGA Professional

"Golf Smart can help you with the other half of your game—putting. While I teach the scientifically proven mechanics of the golf putt, Dr. Varcoe will help you with the equally proven psychological skills that allow you to focus mentally and decrease your score permanently."

– Richard Hill
Founder & CEO of Dick Hill Putting Schools

"The psychological skills that Dr. Varcoe has taught in her seminars and included in this book have helped my students at the Golf Learning Center. While I teach the mechanics of the swing, Dr. Varcoe can help you with the mental skills that are such a big part of the game of golf."

– Jon Ebert
PGA Professional & Owner of the Jon Ebert Learning Center

"This book provides that other dimension—the psychology of golf— so often neglected by the average golfer. Marilyn provides a rare insight into the internal drives that make a difference in the ability to score well and enjoy the game of golf."

– Gene Landrum, Ph.D.
Author, Educator, Speaker, Consultant

"Dr. Varcoe's book is a must for every golfer. Her concepts of the mental skills are practical and get results."

–Dr. Ed Palonk
Author, Medical Consultant, Co-partner in *The Golf Doctor Seminars*

"Golf Smart gets down to the guts of how to change your golf. I think these psychological techniques will help any golfer who really wants to play better and smarter golf. The golfer, not the golf course, sets most limits. This book will help golfers remove those limits."

–Bob Phillips, Ph.D.
Clinical and Sports Psychologist

"Marilyn helps you to tap into the minds of the major champions, and see how they have learned the mental skills that have made them winners. These can be related to the amateur golfer at all levels. She can help you the think your way to a better game."

–Tim Rosaforte
Senior Writer, *Golf World Magazine*

Contents

Dedication
to
Gene Sarazen

I decided to dedicate this book to Gene Sarazen during his funeral on May 13, 1999. The moving ceremony and the eloquent tributes, coupled with the friendship that had developed between us, made me realize there was no one who better represented the game of golf—and no one who could better appreciate the importance of golf's mental side.

As one of the world's greatest golfers, Gene truly epitomized the "gentleman's game." A believer in the traditions of the sport, he made golf history himself by winning all four major championships. His legendary "shot heard 'round the world" double eagle in the 1935 Masters ensured his lasting reputation. But he was more than a skilled golfer and a winning player. He was "the Squire," who practiced a respect for the traditions and purity of the game.

Courtesy of Rick Sharp

Sarazen, "The Squire," was a legend who respected the traditions of the olde game of golfe.

Long an admirer of his golfing abilities and golf history, I met Gene Sarazen at Chateau Elan in Atlanta, Georgia, after the 1997 Masters Tournament. We had just watched Tiger Wood achieve his outstanding win and his first green jacket.

When Gene and I subsequently talked about the importance of the mental side of the game, he smiled, a sparkle in his eye, pointed to his head and said, "Golf is a game up here." His immediate and supportive understanding led to a discussion of how the mental game had affected the new young players in this recent Masters Tournament.

On numerous occasions after that, Gene conveyed to me his understanding that golf is all about the mind and how well one uses it. As was his masterful way, he spoke in few words and short and succinct comments, but it became clear to me that Gene's many years in the world of golf had given him a understanding and knowledge of the game far beyond the typical. At 97 years old, his association with the sport had made him a world legend and granted him a deeper wisdom than any of us today. The concepts that I've written about in this book have come from recent research in the psychology of the game, but Gene understood them intuitively. As much as I believe these concepts will prove to be the forefront of the future teaching of golf, I also believe Gene would agree.

Gene's personal side was as memorable as his golfing feats, and he loved to share stories of his associations and friendships with notable and famous people. One of his favorites was the tale of how he gained the insight to invent the sand wedge. He'd become friendly with Howard Hughes around that time and would fly with him in Hughes' private plane. A notable pilot, Hughes was also a good golfer, and the two would often play together. One day as Gene sat next to him in the cockpit, Hughes invited him to pull the stick back to take the plane up.

Courtesy of Mary Ann Sarazen

Gene was always at the forefront of golf instruction and intuitively understood the psychology of the game. He said, "it's all up here"! (pointing to his head)

That small task was enough to prompt Gene's ingenuity. He realized he could apply aerodynamic principles to golf and shape a club head so that, when the bottom of the club hit the sand, it would bounce out. He experimented with a

Courtesy of Rick Sharp

Don Panos annually hosted the Sarazen Open at Chateau Elan in Atlanta, Georgia and many of the world's best professional players payed their respects to the legendary Squire.

number of clubs, soldering the bottoms until he came up with the right angle to achieve the result he wanted. The Wilson Company has been the beneficiary of Gene's intuitive ingenuity since 1922.

Gene also enjoyed telling stories about his old golfing friends Walter Hagen, Bobby Jones, Harry Vardon and

Courtesy of Mary Ann Sarazen

At Gene Sarazen's 97th (and final) birthday party, held February 27, 1999 at the Island Country Club on Marco Island. Gene was bright and alert even through his final weeks, and he always remained up to date with all the happenings in the golf world.

Tommy Armorer and about the way golf used to be. In his later years, he enjoyed a friendship with Donald Panos, Atlanta businessman and owner of Chateau Elan Hotel & Winery. Panos hosted the Sarazen Open there for many years, attracting great golf professionals from around the world. During an afternoon with Gene and Don Panos at Gene's last Sarazen Open in October 1998, I was once again able to discuss the influence of the mental game on the golf pros playing in that tournament. We all agreed that those with mental toughness and mental control of the game always came out as winners.

With Gene's encouragement and understanding, I have included many of the mental principles we had discussed into this book. So it is with heartfelt enthusiasm that I say, "Thanks, Squire. This one's for you."

Career Highlights

- Winner of 38 PGA Tour titles, of which 7 were major championships.
- First professional golfer to win all four Grand Slam titles.
- Member of first Ryder Cup team, in 1927 and continued on in 1929, 1931, 1933, 1935 and 1937.
- Charter member of World Golf Hall of Fame in 1974.
- 1935 Masters Tournament victory is remembered for his famous double eagle.
- 1973, at 71 years of age, a hole-in-one, at Royal Troon, Scotland, during The Open.
- Credited with the invention of the sand wedge.

Gene Sarazen
"The Squire"

Born: February 27, 1902
     Harrison, New York

Died: May 13, 1999

Mass of Christian Burial
Monday, May 17, 1999
San Marco Church, Marco Island, Florida
Interment Marco Island Cemetery

A Special Thanks to Ken Venturi

⚜

Through his wise counsel, based on his many years as a PGA player, TV commentator and legendary analyst of the game of golf, Ken Venturi has made an immeasurable contribution to this book.

Because of his close and long-standing association with the game, I asked him, "What makes a champion golfer?" He explained there are a number of factors that contribute to make a winning combination: talent, training and opportunity, just to name a few. But the one thing that really separates the great golfers from those who are merely good is how well they handle the mental aspects of the game.

This was a lesson Ken learned early on in his golfing career. He had the great good fortune to be taught to play golf by Ben Hogan, who shared with him the three tactics for winning: "out work them; out think them; and out intimidate them." Ben frequently referred to golf as being 20% technique and 80% mental. Byron Nelson, who was also his teacher for a time, agreed wholeheartedly that the key to winning at golf was making a commitment to the mental side of the game.

At the US Open in 1964, Ken had the chance to put those lessons to the ultimate test. Washington was suffering from a blistering heat wave at the time, and he was coming from behind on the last day of the tournament. He recalled clearly that it was only his mental focus that took him through the 36 holes. It was like being in a "mental cocoon." When it was over, he collapsed from heat exhaustion. Later, he found he had lost eight pounds in that single day. But it was his deep state of focused concentration, mental toughness and determination that allowed him to be victorious.

Courtesy of Ken Venturi

Ken Venturi on the 1st tee at the Los Angeles Open in 1959.

In the many years since Ken played the circuit, he's had the chance to work as a sportscaster for CBS, covering numerous tournaments and players. He's spoken with many of the young players on the professional tour and shared with them his ability to look golfing opponents in the eye and let them know how focused and committed he was to winning.

One of the many players with whom Ken has had the chance to talk about the mental game of golf is David Duval, who was a member of the winning 1999 American team at the Ryder Cup. If any team ever showed the importance of conquering the mental aspects of the game, it was this team. Ben Crenshaw and his players truly believed that they would be able to make that comeback to win the Cup. And they did—in glorious style.

Playing with confidence and belief in yourself is one of the mental skills that will help any golfer with the outcome of his game, but it's a winning formula that isn't restricted to this sport. Ken shared with me the philosophy of his friend, Vince Lombardi, who credits his numerous wins with the Green Bay Packers to the confidence and mental toughness of his players.

Ken is now beginning preparations for his next important role as Captain of the President's Cup in October 2000. You can be sure he'll share with his players the importance of the mental skills needed to emerge as winners. Those mental skills, if understood, acquired and practiced, will ultimately make all the difference in your game of golf.

Courtesy of Ken Venturi

Ken Venturi was the winner of the 1964 US Open in Washington D.C.

Acknowledgments

This project has been a passion for me since I was introduced to the game of golf many years ago by my former spouse, Tom Nardozzo. I recognized immediately what a mental game golf can be. Since then, I've been able to apply my skills, knowledge and experience as a practicing psychologist to this sport that can be so elusive and challenging. I've also had the chance to help golfers understand how to use their mind to their best advantage in the game of golf.

I will be forever grateful to the professors and mentors in my excellent psychology doctoral program at Penn State University, for providing me with the theory and knowledge of the cognitive skills that so aptly apply to the mental game of golf. I particularly want to thank Dr. Deb Crews and Dr. Dan Landers at Arizona State for their collegial support. They freely shared with me their original research and outcome data from their outstanding scientific studies with golf. I hope that in making this valuable information available to amateur golfers everywhere I will help them to a better understanding and greater enjoyment of the game.

A very special thank you to Gene Sarazen and his wonderful family, particularly his daughter Mary Ann, for including me in a golfing world that encompasses a circle of so many interesting and fascinating people.

Many thanks also to Ken Venturi for his wisdom, insights and good advice that have directed me toward the completion of this book.

I gratefully appreciate the knowledge, information, and advice of my colleagues who have encouraged me or advised me in this project; in particular, Dr. Patrick Cohn, sports psychologist in Orlando, Florida; Dr. Bob Phillips, clinical and golf psychologist in Norcross, Georgia; and Dr. Mark Frazier, clinical and golf psychologist in Arlington, Illinois.

Others who have encouraged, supported, and provided me direction in this endeavor include Jon Ebert, PGA Golf Professional; Denis Johnson, business adviser; from Edward Jones, Dan Regelski from Florida Gulf Coast University, Small Business Development Program; Dr. Ed Polank, co-partner in *Golf Doctors* Seminars; Dick Hill of Dick Hill Putting Schools; Bob Ornitz, Senior PGA Golf Professional; Rick Sharp, PGA and LPGA photographer; Jason Dubin of *Golf Coasting* magazine; Mike Dubin of TV Channel 7, sports newscaster; Joe Klimas, Channel 10 sportscaster; and Dr. Gene Landrum, author.

Many thanks also to Barb and Jim Weems of Ad Graphics, Tulsa, Oklahoma for their great designs and direction, and to Janina Birtolo for her editing and who provided me with the assistance to get this into print. Thanks also to those who provided me with advice and assistance including Barbara Rudnicki of RCE Enterprises, Elaine Stanley of First Union Bank, Susan Sokol of Smart Marketing, Beth Hagen, business consultant, and Dr. Priscilla Marotta, psychologist and author.

Most importantly, thanks to the many PGA professionals of Southwest Florida, who have challenged and supported me, and to the many avid golfers who have utilized my knowledge, experience, and consult to improve their games.

To my beloved, deceased father,
who always gave me the love and admiration
to accomplish anything.

To my dear mother,
who has encouraged and supported me
in all my dreams.

To my wonderful sons, Jay and Jeff,
who have given me much joy, happiness,
love and support.

Foreword

Golf is a unique and interesting game to learn. For approximately four to five hours, the golfer attempts to hit a ball, which is a little more than one-and-a-half inches in diameter, with a three- to four-foot long club, having a head that is about six inches long. The golfer wraps this club completely around his body, then lashes violently at the ball, expecting to hit the ball squarely, sending it hundreds of yards straight ahead. The object is to get the ball into a four-and-a-quarter inch hole in the minimum number of strokes. Even though they may not spend much time in practice, most golfers get extremely irritated with themselves if they are not able to perform these skills to perfection over the entire four to five hour round.

Needless to say, golf is a very difficult game to learn; however, if properly learned, it can be a very easy game to play. It is a time consuming process, which is comprised of two equally important areas: the physical and the mental.

Beginning golfers are totally consumed with learning the physical, or mechanical, skills of the game. These include learning how to hold the club and how to move the body, swinging the club back and through, coordinating every motion, forming the repetition necessary to consistently make square contact with the ball. If this sounds difficult, it is! Most golfers never get out of the physical area of the game. They'll spend a lifetime trying to perfect a swing and never truly learn how to play golf.

A few golfers have learned that there's more to becoming a good golfer than just being able to hit the ball. They've learned how to take their physical skills, which have become habit through hours of repetition, and apply their mental skills, which enable them to play golf at a much higher level.

Thousands of golf professionals work on the physical side of the game with hundreds of thousands of golfers daily. They teach golfers how to get into the proper positions and tell them if they repeat these motions correctly enough times, they will form the "muscle memory" required to hit good, consistent golf shots. What most golf professionals do *not* teach their students is how to apply these physical skills on the golf course. In other words, they teach their students how to hit the ball but not how to play golf.

Dr. Marilyn Varcoe, in her book, *Golf Smart*, addresses this topic in a very simple and straight-forward manner, which golfers of all ability levels will easily be able to understand and practice. Dr. Varcoe and I have done many seminars together, and, while I've worked on the physical side of golf for many years, it wasn't until my work with her that I truly understood what allows the better player to "rise" to that next level. Her "Seven Secrets" will unlock the potential in all those struggling golfers who are putting out the effort but not achieving the results.

Jon Ebert,
PGA Professional, Syndicated Golf Columnist

Introduction

✦❧✦

olf has understandably been called the "most mental of all games." In a game that can be the most solitary of sports, your mind is your "partner" and plays the greatest role in the success of your game. Whether it is the golfing partner who helps or hinders, however, is up to you.

Consider the following:

"Golf is 20% technique and 80% mental."
                                            – Ben Hogan

"Golf is a game played on a six-inch course—the space between your ears."
                                            – Sam Snead

"In the 260 minutes it takes to play a round of golf, you spend approximately five minutes swinging the golf club. In the remaining 255 minutes, you play golf in your head."
                                            – Dr. Mark Frazier

That golf is so highly mental a game is not new or surprising information. Almost every player, amateur or professional, will agree. Yet what is surprising is that so few golfers, having made that admission, will pay attention to this mental side and begin to address it. They'll spend endless hours practicing and taking instructional lessons, spend hundreds of dollars on new equipment and gadgets, read volumes of books on how to improve their swing—but they'll rarely spend the time needed to develop their mental skills and improve their game.

Most golfers feel comfortable working on the mechanics of their swing. It's easy to fix a physical problem by practicing and doing drills on the range. But how do we correct a mental problem? How do we identify the source of the problem? And how can we make the changes that will reflect the difference by a lowered score?

The answers to those questions are emerging from the field of sports psychology. Researchers, sports psychologists, and clinicians are discovering that certain cognitive skills that had been previously proven effective in working with mental health clients can also enhance performance in most sports. As we have begun to understand the importance of the mind-body connection, we have been able to develop techniques and practices, supported by scientific study, to help athletes improve their performance by effectively using their minds.

As a clinical and sports psychologist myself, I've seen this research validated with my own clients. The way we think is truly the way we feel and behave.

Researchers at several universities, particularly Arizona State, have more recently begun to study how the psychological-cognitive-behavioral interventions that have proven to be effective in facilitating general sports performance might best be applied to the game of golf. By studying and understanding how the elite golfer executes his golf stroke, researchers have identified interventions to improve performance. Among the most effective techniques are (1) intensity regulation and relaxation techniques; (2) imagery and visualization; (3) goal setting, mental preparation, and practice;

(4) cognitive strategies; and (5) attentional focus and concentration. These skills, when learned and practiced by golfers, have been shown to make a difference and lower scores.

These techniques and skills are what I've identified as "The Seven Secrets of the Mental Game of Golf." By understanding and using them, you can influence your performance, build your confidence in the game, and guarantee both greater success and enjoyment in your game of golf. You'll also build your mental strength and toughness, allowing you increased confidence and the ability to respond well in any golfing situation.

Golf is ultimately an individual sport and you are largely in control of its outcome. On the course, there is no place to hide and no teammates to share the blame. Hitting that small two-and-a-half-inch ball with a 36-inch club and a four-inch clubhead is an incredible and challenging feat. It is a game of precision and commitment that requires perfection—regardless of the imperfect conditions you may face on any given course and day. This challenge creates an addiction that keeps golfers continually coming back for more, with an insatiable desire to conquer the game. But the more you apply the passion to perform better, the more you can become frustrated with mistakes. Players who lack confidence and commitment or have a negative attitude will really struggle with their game.

It need not be a downward cycle, however. Sports psychologists have found that being more relaxed, keeping a positive attitude, remaining totally focused, being committed to the outcome and becoming more confident improves athletic performance. The same can be true for you.

In the chapters that follow I'll explain the psychological concepts, techniques, strategies and skills that are emerging from the scientific research into the psychology of sports. These proven elements can help players at all levels, from those with high handicaps to professional golfers, to improve their game and gain the composure, control and mental strength to perform their best. Remember that "every golf shot begins in the mind and the body doesn't lie for the brain."

This book will teach you to use your mind to its best advantage in golf and in your life. You will experience a better enjoyment and pleasure of your game when you begin to utilize and practice the concepts contained herein.

Secret 1
Confidence

*"Confidence is everything in golf...
It's confidence that makes a good player
into a great player and eventually a champion."*

– Fred Couples

Confidence

*"It's the young players with confidence who will be
at the top of the leader board."*

– Gene Sarazen

onfidence is unequivocally the most important
ingredient in mastering the mind game of golf.
Feeling confident about your abilities is THE
essential key to playing great golf. With it, you'll be able to
focus full, clear attention on each and every shot and be free
to apply the correct strategies. Without it, you'll be
continually second-guessing yourself and inadvertently
setting yourself up for failure and disappointment. No one
can be successful without it. Confidence is *knowing* you can
do something. It's the belief in your own abilities.

Confidence is not something you are born with but, rather,
a learned habit. A confident attitude is something that you
can acquire by mastering the skills of the games. If you are
mentally tough, you can stay confident even when things
are not going well for you.

A good example of the difference confidence can make
occurred at the 1999 Ryder Cup. I was fortunate enough to
be at the Brookline Country Club in Boston to watch the

team during the week of play. The American team was so far behind on the last day that no one ever would have believed they could have made the greatest comeback in golf history. But, before that match, Ben Crenshaw said on TV, "I know we are going to win!" The doubters became believers when the American team fulfilled Crenshaw's prophecy.

The team members truly had the confidence, mental strength, and belief in their abilities. They knew they would win. And that's just what confidence can do for you. I spoke with many of them after their victory and they never doubted the final outcome. It can become a self-fulfilling prophecy. Believe you can and you will. Believe you can't and you won't. I believe every one of those golfers at the Ryder Cup had the same skill level and physical ability. The difference was in how they mentally handled the game, specifically in how confident and determined they were to make that victory happen

When you're on the golf course, your confidence is based on your belief in yourself and your abilities. When you prepare to make a golf shot and you believe you have the ability to make a good shot, if you feel confident it's much more likely that the shot will be successful. If you stand over the ball and begin to doubt your abilities, you obviously are not confident, and the chances of the shot being successful are diminished.

The keys to confidence is practice, experience, and successful performances. When you practice a skill long enough, hard enough and correctly, you will develop a level of comfort in your performance that exudes confidence.

Confidence during competition

How can you maintain confidence while playing in difficult competitive circumstances? Do you think the 1999 Americans' Ryder Cup victory was just chance?

Courtesy of Rick Sharp

Gene Sarazen has been able to masterfully develop this skill of confidence over his years of playing the game and is a model for all young players today.

Performing well in the competitive arena is certainly more difficult because the normal level of comfort experienced during regular play may be compromised by the additional stress of a tournament. To play with confidence you must be able to *TRUST* your abilities. Such inhibitors of a free-flowing swing as indecision, fear, hesitation, tentativeness, doubt and over-concern with result, will disappear with the feeling of trust in yourself.

You can develop this trust with the mental practice of specific "game-like" situations. While you practice, imagine that you are playing in the club championship match. Try to imagine the actual experiences you would feel during the height of competition. Learn to relax and feel comfortable and confident in that moment. As your golf teachers have told you, "Trust your swing." Building trust and confidence will make the difference in your mental toughness, even during competitive play.

Consider the following stories of competitive matches. When regulation play ended at the 1987 Masters, Steve Ballesteros, Greg Norman and Larry Mize were in a three-way tie for first place, setting the stage for a dramatic finish. During the playoff, the scoring system was changed from medal to match play—the golfers would have to keep pace with one another on each hole or be eliminated. This change clearly favored Ballesteros, who had a reputation for playing well under intense pressure. Of the three, he was the only one who had won the Masters previously, so he presumably knew what it would take.

Unfortunately, Ballesteros three-putted on the first hole of the playoff and was eliminated from the match. A look of disbelief swept over his face. The fans didn't realize it at the time, but his confidence was shattered. He later admitted it took him almost two years to recover his short-putt confidence fully.

Greg Norman experienced the other side of confidence at the 1990 Doral Open's sudden death playoff, when he

Courtesy of Rick Sharp

Payne Stewart had a consistent easy flowing swing he could trust, even in the most competitive situations.

chipped in for an eagle on the first hole. The shot gave him the tournament victory. Afterwards, he said, "I was lining up my chip and Bruce (my caddie) said, 'Chip it in, you're due.' I said, 'OK, sure.' He gave me that extra shot of confidence I needed."

Finally, there is Ben Hogan, considered one of the finest golfers ever to play the game. Surprisingly, he was plagued by self-doubt during the first 15 years of his career. Even if things were going well on the course, he would always worry about what might go wrong. It was only after Hogan learned how to keep up his confidence that the self-doubting finally stopped and he was able to reach his potential.

The psychological research on confidence

At this point, you might be tempted to think, "That's all well and good, but I'm not a Greg Norman or Ben Hogan." But before you dismiss all these reports of the importance of confidence, you might want to know about the exciting new research that points to a scientific basis for these anecdotes. Confidence, it appears, really **is** all in your head.

At Arizona State University, Dr. Deb Crews shared with me her research findings, which were recently reported at the World Congress of Golf at St. Andrews, Scotland. Working with a group of tour players, Dr. Crews set out to determine the psycho-physiological indicators of confidence, using EEG tests to measure brain activity during the golf stroke. The results of the investigative study indicated that confident putts were characterized by a lower level of activity in the brain.

Dr. Crews discovered that, when a golfer is confident about a putt, he/she can play more automatically and smoothly—without the distractions of negative self-talk and/

or over-analysis of the shot. Have you ever noticed how actions you are sure of feel effortless? That's confidence at work. And when confidence is working at an optimal level, the results tend to be more consistently positive.

For example, consider your own everyday experience of learning to drive a car. There was so much to think about! It seemed you'd never get all the shifting, accelerating, watching, steering, turning and braking coordinated. But one day it all suddenly slipped into a groove, and you were driving down the highway as if you'd driven all your life.

Dr. Crews' study showed these exact same principles at work in a player's golf stroke, with a corresponding decrease in alpha brain activity. Having trust and confidence in your stoke is the best guarantee of that dropped ball in the hole. And the perfect stroke is yours to accomplish if you will quiet your talking brain and believe in your own abilities.

Misconceptions about confidence

So how do you build confidence? Let's start by dispelling some myths that have grown up around the concept.

In a discussion about confidence, Jack Nicklaus was once quoted as saying, "You just have it and you go out and do it. There's no developing it." It's difficult to imagine that someone who knows the game as well as Nicklaus can believe that a golfer could not develop confidence, and I suspect his comment was taken out of context. Many golfers, however, unfortunately believe that confidence is truly a "have or have not" situation.

Let's examine this proposition. If confidence is a matter of having or not having and you are fortunate enough to be in the "have" group, then apparently confidence is yours for life. Yet we've already seen that was not the case for Seve Ballesteros after the 1987 Masters. Indeed, Ballesteros would probably argue that a golfer's confidence can come and go far too easily.

Courtesy of Rick Sharp

Jack Nicklaus understands the importance of confidence in his game and has clearly demonstrated it over the years.

40

Conversely, if you believe in the have or have not theory and you place yourself among the "have nots," then apparently you're destined to doubt your abilities throughout your golfing career.

The fallacy of this attitude should be readily apparent. Ben Hogan is a classic example of a golfer who learned how to build his confidence and eventually have plenty of it. The reality is that any golfer can build confidence. Any golfer can play with confidence. It's simply a matter of learning how and then working on it.

Another popular misconception held by many golfers is that confidence is determined by how well you have been playing recently. If you have played well during the preceding rounds, your confidence is high. If you did not play well, then your confidence is low. A quick glance at the sports section of the newspaper clears up this misconception. What you'll find is that the scores of the tour players can vary by 10 or more strokes from day to day.

The successful tour players, those who play with confidence, allow yesterday's score to influence their confidence today ONLY if they like the score. They'll then take yesterday's game and use it to build confidence for today's round. If yesterday's score was unacceptable, they discard it. They don't give it a chance to affect their confidence. Tour players who are NOT selective about how they let their scores influence their confidence spend a lot of weekends at home.

When you play well, use your scores to build your confidence. When you don't play well, don't dwell on it. Your confidence needs to be protected. Take care of your confidence as you do your clubs and equipment. Store it with pride and pleasure!

Building confidence

One of the most important factors in building and maintaining confidence is self-talk. All golfers engage in conversation with themselves for a good part of every round. What you say to yourself during those conversations can have a dramatic effect on your confidence.

As you prepare to make an approach shot, you can increase your confidence if you remind yourself that you're sure of the distance, sure of the target and that you know how to and will swing smoothly. Remind yourself that you are a good player and that you can easily make this shot. You will increase the likelihood of doing just that if you give yourself positive self-statements.

The opposite is also true. Let's say you're preparing to hit a tee shot. You will lessen your confidence if you tell yourself that the landing area is too small, that there's trouble on the left or that recently you've tended to hook your shot. These kinds of statements will make the stroke more difficult than necessary. Remember: you have control over what you say to yourself. Keep the conversations positive, and your confidence stays high.

Golfers who underestimate the influence of their self-talk are making a costly mistake. Do you often see players who shoot low scores talk disparagingly to themselves? But I'll bet you've seen plenty of high scoring golfers who are super-critical of themselves. Unfortunately, the golf courses are full of them.

The power of self-talk

To understand how powerfully your self-talk can affect your confidence, consider the "yips." This neurological syndrome is like a panic attack and can get so bad that you stand helplessly shaking whenever you have to putt.

A case of the yips doesn't develop overnight. It takes time, and there is a cumulative effect. A negative conversation is followed by negative statements, which are then followed by more negative conversation. When golfers engage in enough of these conversations, they seriously harm their confidence. Some of the world's best putters have become nervous wrecks within three feet of the cup, simply because of the way they talked to themselves.

Courtesy of Rick Sharp

Vijah Singh is a good putter who recognizes the importance of positive self-talk throughout the game.

Some of the time you're aware of the conversations you have with yourself and some of the time you're not, so you have to be careful. Self-talk occurs on both the conscious and subconscious levels. When it occurs subconsciously, you harm yourself without even knowing it. Therefore, it's vital to be positive and encouraging in your self-talk ALL THE TIME. When you're playing golf, make it a habit to be your own best friend. Golf instructor Harvey Penick once said, "The golfing area of the brain is a fragile thing that is terribly susceptible to suggestion." Remember Penick's words and keep your self-talk the type that will build and not destroy your confidence.

The cycle of success

When you're successful at what you're doing, your confidence and trust in yourself will naturally increase. And as your confidence builds, you will be even more successful. This, in turn, makes you even more confident. Success builds confidence, and confidence builds success, a victorious cycle rather than a vicious one.

One of the ways Ben Hogan built his confidence was by replaying, in his mind, his great shots. When Hogan was really happy with a shot, he would replay it for himself repeatedly. If he had time, he would do so right after making the shot. If not, he would replay it later in the round. Hogan referred to this strategy as "retasting the sweetness." Replaying the shot let him re-experience his successes, and, as we know, success breeds confidence.

After you hit a great shot, remember to replay it for yourself, over and over. Recall how it felt, what you saw and what you heard.

Whatever your handicap, there are many ways to feel success in golf. It's simply a matter of setting realistic goals for yourself and then accomplishing them with a positive attitude.

Mental practice tips

One of the statistics kept by the PGA is driving accuracy, or the percentage of time that the player's tee shot hits the fairway. The leaders in this category usually make the fairway around 75% of the time. Do you want to feel more confident with your driver? Calculate the number of times your drives hit the fairway or the green during a round of golf and watch your percentages increase. Before long, you'll be hitting more golf targets and increasing confidence in your game.

Do you want to be more confident with your short game? Set up a similar program to improve your putting gradually. Here's one way of doing that: Set four balls two feet directly north of the cup. Keep stroking balls until you sink four in a row. Now, move the balls two feet south of the cup and keep putting until you sink four in a row from there. Do the same east and west of the cup. Once you come full circle, move the balls out to the three-foot range and follow the same procedure.

Keeping in mind that being successful is what is most important, you can gradually increase the distances of your putts. With enough practice, you'll be making a lot of putts, and your success in your short game will increase your confidence level in your ability to play a great round of golf.

If you'd like to increase your confidence with your longer shots, you can experiment on the practice range. Select a target that is about the distance you normally hit your driver. Next, set aside three piles of four balls. Hit the first pile and keep track of how many shots come within 10 feet of your target. Do the same with the remaining two piles of balls. Make it your goal to have more balls within 10 feet of the target from the last pile than any other pile. Keep trying until you succeed.

Always have goals in mind as you practice your game on the range, and always remember your successful shots and let go of the bad ones.

Keep those skills sharp

As seen in Dr. Crews' study, good skills, well ingrained, are fundamental to producing consistent play and building confidence. You want to get to the point where the basics are automatic, and the practice range is a good place to acquire and keep that sense of habit.

Golfing instructor Jon Ebert teaches new students that, if they practice 50 repetitions of a swing for 30 days, they will have that swing grooved. It will be there and all you'll need to do is call on it whenever you want it—automatically. So take the time for regular practice. You'll be glad you did.

When you're on the course, remember to keep your expectations realistic. How you define a successful shot is an important factor in building and maintaining confidence. Hitting a 250-yard drive down the center of the fairway is obviously a great shot! But, depending on your skill level, this may not always happen. Similarly, all golfers would like to one-putt each hole, but is that realistic for you? Having unrealistic expectations can undermine both your game and your confidence.

Sometimes, success is hitting your ball out of a bush and back onto the fairway. Sometimes, it's a shot that clears a tree and allows you a chance to par the hole. There are even times when a bogey is a good score.

Remember, when you're successful, your confidence goes up. The more consistently you play well, the more you'll believe in your ability to be a good golfer. When your goals are commensurate with your skills, you'll be successful more often, giving your confidence a boost and increasing both your success and enjoyment of the game!

Courtesy of Rick Sharp

Craig Stadler has said, "Confidence is everything. From there it's a small step to winning."

47

SUMMARY TIPS:

The benefits of confidence

1) Confidence arouses positive emotions. When feeling confident, you are more likely to remain calm and relaxed under pressure.

2) Confidence facilitates concentration. When you feel confident, your mind is free to focus on the task at hand. When you lack confidence, you tend to worry about how well you are doing.

3) Confidence affects goals. Confident golfers set challenging goals and pursue them. Confidence helps you to play your best game.

4) Confidence increases effort. How much effort a golfer extends and how long he persists in pursuit of a goal depends largely on how much confidence he has in his ability to achieve that goal.

5) Confidence affects psychological momentum. Golfers with confidence are able to reach their optimal performance levels and play "in the zone."

Reminders to help your game

1) Remember the good shots and forget the bad ones. The latter steals your energy and undermines your confidence. Put bad shots to the back of your mind and selectively recall only the good shots.

2) Stay in the present with each shot. Worrying about the past or the future will not help your game. Simply make the best shot you can at the time and then go on and do it again.

3) Keep stress levels to a minimum by keeping the perspective that the outcome of your golf game is not a life-threatening event. Golf is a game to be enjoyed!

4) Don't try to cognitively control the mechanics of your swing. Trying to steer or guide the club to the target will ruin your stroke. Excessive muscular involvement in the swing will only ruin your natural stroke.

5) Develop the skills of mental toughness by mentally practicing stressful events in competition and selectively recall those situations where you came through when the heat was on.

6) Keep a journal or notebook for data collection of your good shots with each club. When subsequently using a club, recall the recorded plays and build your confidence to re-create the same event each time.

Secret 2
Concentration

"When I'm in this state, everything is pure,
vividly clear. I'm in a cocoon of concentration."

– Arnold Palmer

Concentration

"When I played well, I felt it was like being in a zone, of being almost hypnotized."

– Ken Venturi

"You play your best golf by just reacting to the target. If you are focused on the target, you aren't thinking about anything bad happening."

– Davis Love III

The sense of being in "a mental cocoon" noted by Ken Venturi, Davis Love and Arnold Palmer is a vivid description of the highly focused concentration that is vital in most sports, but it is of special importance when it comes to golf. Unlike other sports, golf requires you to initiate action, not just to react to the game that is happening around you. When you step up to a shot, you alone are in control, and to do your best you need to be focused enough that the birds in the trees or the maintenance cart rumbling by don't pull your attention away and distract you from the shot at hand.

Definition and style

What do we mean by concentration in golf? Dr. Michael Maloney, one of my mentors at Penn State University, has studied concentration in athletes. What he found led him to develop this definition, which I find particularly appropriate and accurate: "To concentrate means to center, to become totally absorbed or focused on a specific point, task or theme of action, free from any irrelevant internal or external distraction, yet tuned in to those cues most relevant to peak performance."

Courtesy of Rick Sharp

Arnold Palmer has learned to use focused concentration during the critical parts of his game.

While that definition details what concentration is, it's important to realize that, in golf, there are different styles of concentrating. Some golfers, known as "grinders," are able to maintain a high level of concentration throughout a round. Whether they are hitting a shot, walking down the fairway, lining up a putt or stopping for a drink of water, they are able to focus on their game all of the time. Seve Ballesteros and Nick Faldo are examples of golfers who are totally focused. Ballesteros has explained that entering his mental cocoon ensures every shot gets his full individual attention.

Sam Snead, who played many big matches against Ben Hogan, was convinced that Hogan would go into a "trance" on the first tee and not come out of it until the end of the round. Snead may have been more right than he realized. The stories about Hogan's deep level of concentration are legendary—including one in which his wife, Valerie, came up and spoke to him during a round. Afterward, Hogan couldn't remember even seeing her on the course. Hogan was obviously a disciplined golfer who could directly control his level of concentration and remain mentally "tough" throughout the round.

Snead, on the other hand, liked to mix business with pleasure. Like Fuzzy Zoeller and Jack Nicklaus, he could adjust his level of concentration to the situation. When it's time to make a shot, their concentration is intense. Between shots, they allow their thoughts to wander and seem to enjoy their surroundings. Nicklaus has even been known to pause in the middle of the British Open to sketch a green he wanted to include in a course he was designing!

Maintaining a high level of focused concentration for extended periods of time requires an incredible amount of energy, and most golfers would find it exhausting to concentrate for the entire four and a half hours it takes to play a round. Such intensity can even be counterproductive, producing stress and ultimately burning you out. And, as Snead, Zoeller and Nicklaus have shown, it's not necessary to be focused all the time.

Courtesy of Rick Sharp

Payne Stewart always looked like he was enjoying the game and his surroundings.

Find the style of concentration that works best for you. Experiment, on and off the course, with focusing on one thing for different amounts of time. Note when and why your attention starts to wander. After some trial and error, you will discover the individual style that is your ideal.

Two steps to concentration

One of the greatest differences between the weekend golf player and the touring professional is the ability to concentrate. Elite players have learned that to play their best they must give each shot their COMPLETE attention. Weekend players are much more likely to bring along "excess baggage" in the form of domestic or business concerns, evening plans, past mistakes and the like. Unfortunately, when you allow your mind to wander away from the shot at hand to these extraneous and, at the moment, irrelevant thoughts, something always seems to go wrong with your game.

The good news is that concentration is a skill you can develop by practicing two simple steps: (1) clearing you mind and (2) immersing yourself in the shot.

Clear your mind

The mind works most effectively when it's free of distractions. As you prepare for a golf shot, the first step is to get rid of mind clutter. Forget what's going on at home, forget what has happened at the office and forget what you have to do after the round. Let go of past errors—like that "easy" putt you missed on the previous hole. If the thought doesn't have to do with the shot you are preparing to make now, put it out of your mind.

That advice, of course, can sometimes be easier said than done. Your mind can be as contrary as a rebellious youngster when told not to do something. As soon as you tell it not to think about something, it can find no other more pressing or interesting thought. You tell yourself, for example, "I am not thirsty, I am not thirsty," only to discover your thirst grows with each declaration.

Courtesy of Rick Sharp

Hale Irwin has the ability to concentrate completely and stay focused even with the distractions of big crowds during tournaments.

People who are just beginning the practice of self-hypnosis or meditation often fall into this very trap. Told to empty their minds, they push at intruding thoughts only to meet increasing resistance. This is why we will often suggest that beginners start by concentrating on or staring at something external. We know that pushing thoughts away aggressively is counterproductive. If you give your mind something to fill it totally, other thoughts will wither on their own from lack of attention.

Immerse yourself in your shot

By gently ignoring extraneous thoughts, you can begin to focus in on the shot at hand. You can slip into a "coma" by getting focused on the shot you are preparing to make. The shot is the only thing you should think about now. It is all that matters in this moment.

We now need to consider the two types of concentration, as both come into play while you are immersing yourself in the shot. These two types of concentration are indicative of the two sides of your brain, and both are needed in the game of golf. You've no doubt heard the terms left-brained and right-brained. The left brain governs analytical, detail oriented tasks. The right-brain governs intuitive, more artistic pursuits. The corresponding types of concentration are disciplined concentration and flow concentration.

Disciplined concentration occurs during a golfer's preshot routine. It concerns analysis of course conditions, gauging the effects of weather, selection of shot and club, aiming at the target, alignment of the body to the intended line of flight and body posture.

Flow concentration is the intuitive subconscious sense that occurs during the swing. It is being fully absorbed in the present task, with attention finely attuned to the shifting demands of the moment. It is also trusting your instincts and your grooved swing.

By being aware of these two different yet mutually necessary types of concentration and cultivating the ability to shift smoothly between them, you will be able to give your best to each shot.

Playing in "The Zone"

Have you ever gotten so caught up in a task that you became oblivious to the passage of time? Everything went smoothly and you could do no wrong. You felt alive and vital, and all that mattered in the world was the work in which you were so totally involved. When you finished and looked at the clock, you couldn't believe how much you had accomplished and how well it was done. It seemed like magic.

That kind of experience can happen with just about any endeavor, but when it happens in sports it's known as playing in the zone. You've no doubt seen professional athletes, like David Duval, when they're in the zone. You may even have been fortunate enough to have had the experience yourself.

Playing in the zone is the ultimate exhilaration in golf. When you're in the zone, you're entirely focused in the present moment. You feel totally confident about your abilities, have no doubts or fears and are completely relaxed—both physically and mentally. In short, it is sheer bliss.

While we don't understand everything about the zone, we do that accomplished players get into the zone more frequently than average players do and they stay there longer. This would suggest that a certain amount of self-trust in your athletic abilities is a prerequisite to entering the zone. The further hypothesis, to which most scientists subscribe, is that the ability to concentrate deeply and relax is what allows players into the zone.

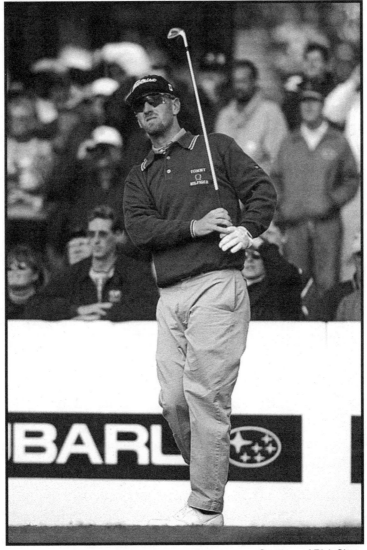

Courtesy of Rick Sharp

David Duval has learned to relax and play in the zone.

Since we would all like to play in the zone, a good place to start is by honing your basic skills, grooving them until they become instinctive and trustworthy. Having trust in your abilities clears away worries that can distract you from the deep concentration and deep relaxation you need to make your best shots. You can also help yourself along the path to the zone by learning to recognize and combat the deterrents to concentration.

Deterrents to concentration

Concentration can be hard to maintain, especially over the course of a full round of golf. As we've already discussed, most golfers find it far more advantageous to develop the ability to slip in and out of concentrated states. But there are also specific hazards that can intrude and wreak havoc with your concentration, even if you're not grinding. If you are aware of them, you can then work to maintain control over them.

Anxiety

When you're feeling tense and anxious during play, your concentration level will decrease. Often, golfers become stressed about their scores, the slow players ahead or the pressure of golfers pushing from behind. Sometimes, the anxiety springs from events in your life that have nothing to do with the golf game you're playing. Regardless of its source, anxiety levels can climb so high they interfere with your enjoyment of the game and the moment at hand.

In this state, it's easy to lose sight of the fact that you're on the course to enjoy yourself. Golf courses are beautiful places, and nature can be a great soother. Be aware of what's around you and let it remind you of why you came there in the first place.

Boredom

Golf pros who play a great deal of golf and retirees who "live" on the golf course can find the greatest threat to their game is the feeling of boredom when playing with others who may not be at the same ability level. Most golfers don't get enough chance to play to become bored, but if you do—or even if you just get too much chance to play the same course over and over—you may find yourself becoming "brain dead" from too much play.

Boredom can lead to playing without concentration, feeling and mental imagery. To eliminate the problem the player must feel challenged and psyched up for the match. (Techniques for doing this will be more fully covered in the Intensity Regulation chapter.) You can accomplish this with motivational self-statements and/or such challenges as trying to accomplish more difficult shots.

Distraction

Other golfers, slow play, golf course maintenance crews, the weather and other environmental elements can frequently distract golfers from their focus and lessen their concentration level.

Obviously, there's not much you can do about a breeze that kicks up or a bird that starts to chirp. You simply can't eliminate all the noise outside. But you can eliminate it from your consciousness. Remember to immerse yourself in your shot fully, gently crowding out the unnecessary by filling your mind with what's in front of you. Develop tunnel vision, so that you can remain totally focused throughout your shot.

Pressure

In a pressure situation, golfers can easily make mistakes. They'll rush their pre-shot routine, make a hasty—and subsequently poor—club selection or pay too little attention to course management. Any of these are signs that the pressure is negatively affecting their concentration level.

In a later chapter, I'll discuss specific relaxation techniques you can use on and off the course, to lessen the impact of pressure (and anxiety). But the most important thing to keep in mind in these or any tense situations is that focusing clearly on and immersing yourself fully in the shot at hand will always help.

SUMMARY TIPS:

In summary, to play your best golf, be aware of the factors that can threaten your concentration; maintain your attentional focus throughout your pre-shot routine; and remember to have fun!

Concentration tip #1

The human mind is capable of concentrating at many different levels. Think of a range from 1 to 10. Level 1 is perfect when you're sitting in the car at a railroad crossing, waiting for the train to go by. Level 3 is just right for enjoying dinner with friends or taking a leisurely walk. You may want to be at Level 7 or 8 during an office meeting. But when it's time to hit a golf ball, you want your concentration at Level 10. The more skilled you become at concentrating, the closer you are to golf's ultimate exhilaration.

Concentration tip #2

From his research on concentration in athletes, Dr. Michael Maloney of Penn State has come up with the following advice trio for golfers:

1) Concentrate on *positive thoughts*

2) Concentrate on *current events*

3) Concentrate on *positive self-suggestions.*

Concentrating on positive thoughts means thinking about the shot you want to make—in clear, positive terms. When faced with a water hazard, don't think, "Stay out of the water," as that just gives your mind a picture of water that it could interpret as the target you want to hit. Instead, try thinking something like, "Hit it straight down the fairway."

Concentrating on current events simply means remaining in the present moment. Don't let your mind wander to things unrelated to the shot at hand. Focus in on what's happening around you only to the extent that it will affect your shot.

Concentrating on positive self-suggestions is the most obvious of this trio. This is not the time to berate yourself for weaknesses you feel you have or for past mistakes. This is the time to remind yourself of all your strong points.

Concentration tip #3

You may also find that it helps your concentration if you take the time for a mental warm up before playing. Just as warming up on the practice green benefits your muscles and physical skills, warming up your mind will make it easier to slip into a focused state when you need to do so. You may want to start on the drive over, listening to some soothing music and remembering particularly enjoyable experiences you've had golfing before. When you get to the course, give yourself sufficient time to disengage your mind from whatever activity you were doing before. Relax, breathe deeply, take in your surroundings—and get ready to play!

Secret 3
Imagery

"You can't do it unless you've imagined it first."

– Peter Jacobsen
(about a six foot putt)

Imagery

"Before every shot, I go to the movies inside my head. Here is what I see. First, I see the ball where I want it to finish, nice and white and sitting up high on the bright green grass. Then, I see the ball going there, its path and trajectory and even its behavior on landing. The next scene shows me making the kind of swing that will turn the previous image into reality. These home movies are a key to my concentration and to my positive approach to every shot."

– Jack Nicklaus

As the quotation above illustrates, Jack Nicklaus believes that rehearsing his shots in his mind before he actually swings is critical to his success. In fact, Nicklaus has said that hitting a good golf shot is 10% swing, 40% stance and setup and 50% the mental picture of how the swing should occur.

What Nicklaus discovered mirrors what scientists have found: imagery is one of the most effective tools among world class athletes for improving sports performance. Researchers have found that the mind-body connection is so strong that the body will literally create whatever picture the mind presents to it.

You may have heard several different terms to describe an athlete's mental preparation for competition, including visualization, mental rehearsal and mental practice. These are all forms of imagery, which is the process of creating an

POSITIVE IMAGERY

Visualize the shot and tell yourself that
"This shot is going straight to the pin."

experience in the mind. Imagery involves recalling from memory pieces of information stored from experience and shaping these pieces into meaningful pictures. These experiences are essentially a product of your memory that you

VISUALIZATION

A good golfer is confident and visualizes herself
successfully making the shot.

experienced internally by recalling and reconstructing previous events. Imagery can be viewed as a form of simulation. It is similar to a real sensory experience, but the entire experience occurs in the mind.

The power of imagery is well illustrated by the story of the Vietnam War POW who survived his captivity by playing a round of golf in his head each day. He took great care to make the imaginary round as detailed as possible, actually walking the course in his head, noting his surroundings and closely focusing on each and every shot. After he was released and had the chance to return to the golf course, he shot a 74!

I first understood the effectiveness of imagery when I began applying this technique to my former spouse to help improve his game. Before a big tournament match, I would assist him with his visualization by using the golf score card of the holes to be played. I would take him through the round, hole by hole and have him image himself being successful with each shot. He could shave six strokes off his score just by these sessions.

I also had a golfing client who was temporarily unable to play because he was recovering from an operation. I had him mentally practice the game instead, an exercise that helped strengthen his neural pathways so that when he returned to the game he hadn't lost ground. He was able to continue to enjoy golf even when he was temporarily disabled.

The strengthening of neural pathways through imagery has also been scientifically proven. In a study of skiers, researchers found that having the athletes imagine their movements on the ski slope resulted in a strengthening of their muscles. Imagery improved the movements the skiers made when actually skiing. Golfers, like Ernie Els have said, "you can trust your muscle memory to take over."

What makes imagery even more exciting and promising is that our minds can also image or picture events even if we haven't actually experienced them. While imagery relies heavily on memory, we can build an image

Courtesy of Rick Sharp

Ernie Els has said, "You can trust your muscle memory to take over."

from several different parts of memory. Thus, football quarterbacks can view films of the defense they will be facing and, through imagery, see themselves using certain offensive sets and strategies to offset the specific defensive alignments. To take this one step further, a golfer preparing for a tournament on a new course can walk that course prior to play and then use the experience to imagine himself playing a successful round there.

Making the most of imagery

While it's true that the mind thinks in pictures, scientists have found that imagery is most effective when **all** the senses are involved. Imagery uses the kinesthetic, auditory, tactile and olfactory senses. All are potentially important in the execution of the golf swing. Using more than one sense helps to create more vivid images, making the experience even more real.

The kinesthetic sense is particularly important to athletes because it involves the sensation of bodily position or movement that arises form the stimulation of sensory nerve endings in muscles, joints and tendons. In essence, the kinesthetic sense is the feeling of our body as it moves in different positions. As the study on skiers showed, imagining those movements can result in actual improvement in the movements.

Let's take the example of trying to perfect your golf swing. Your goal is to make your swing as fluid and natural as possible, to achieve a consistent and accurate drive off the tee. To accomplish this, you take a bucket of balls to the driving range and practice your swing continually, trying to automate (i.e. "groove') your swing. Through this physical activity, you are strengthening the neural pathways that control the muscles related to your golf swing. But, as the skiers proved, you can also strengthen these pathways by imagining you are executing a perfect swing. Through the imagery, your body believes that you are actually practicing the swing and responds by programming your muscles and preparing your body to perform.

Courtesy of Rick Sharp

Payne Stewart had grooved a swing that was fluid and natural. Imagery was the most powerful mental tool in his golf bag.

Golf instructor Jon Ebert utilizes this principle with his students by videotaping their swings and having them watch the resulting tape. By seeing themselves in action, in addition to physically practicing, the golf students have two sensory impulses to build their subsequent images.

You can add to these two senses by also being aware of and recalling the sound of the club hitting the golf ball and remembering how it feels to hit a solid shot. The more senses you can involve, the clearer the picture your mind will be able to create during imagery.

Promising possibilities

While a variety of mental training techniques (including imagery, relaxation and hypnosis) have been used to enhance golf performance, few comparison studies exist to determine the effectiveness level of each, particularly as applied to golf. One technique that has been researched at Arizona State that holds great promise is the use of dichotic listening during the execution of a swing. It is known as "Peripheral Processing" (PP).

PP introduces mental process instructions through two separate taped stories, each fed into one ear, with background music. It has been used to study hemispheric differentiation, to understand attention and to predict performance. A recent study by Dr, Crews has indicated it can have valuable application for golfers.

The purpose of Crews study was to examine the effects of PP training on golf performance and psychological state, and to compare the effects with such other techniques as hypnosis and relaxation music. Psychological variables (i.e. self esteem, anxiety and self efficacy) and performance variables (putting and full swing) were assessed over a two-week period.

The immediate results showed significant interaction with all three methods. Putts made increased for advanced golfers with hypnosis, for intermediate golfers using PP and music and for beginning golfers with just music. This suggests that at different skill levels different psychological techniques may be more effective.

Overall, PP produced consistent positive effects in performance and in psychological state. Future research may help us determine if those effects result from the messages on the PP tape or from the tape's ability to reduce distracting self-talk. This kind of research on golf will continue to provide us with valuable techniques that will improve our game.

Obstacles to effective imagery

One of the things most golfers **don't** do is to employ imagery even during practice. This can lessen both the technique's effectiveness and your ability to remember to do it during play. You will want to get in the habit of imagining each and every shot before you take it—just as Nicklaus does. And the best way to develop this habit is to do it over and over, until it becomes automatic. By using imagery during practice, you are helping to strengthen the skill and to establish it as part of your normal routine.

Another complaint I often hear from golfing clients is that they sometimes have trouble visualizing themselves making a shot, particularly if it's one they haven't been able to make before. If you have that problem, don't despair of ever developing the skill. Researchers have found that modeling and vicarious experience accounts for half of our learning. You can begin by watching golf tournaments and taking in the pictures of your favorite players. Notice how they are able to complete 30-foot putts or hit a perfect drive. By storing those pictures in your memory, you can recall them as the basis for future imagery. Eventually, you will be able to substitute a picture of yourself in place of them and mentally see yourself playing the way you want to play.

Psychologists and golf pros agree that imagery is the most powerful mental tool in your golf bag. Incorporating positive mental images will provide a blueprint for your shot. Given that blueprint, your body will respond. What's more, imagery can help enhance a variety of other skills to improve performance and facilitate the learning of new techniques and strategies. Golfers who want to better their game would be wise to take heed.

IMAGERY TIP #1

Uses of Imagery

Golfers can employ imagery skills to achieve a number of different benefits:

1) **Improve concentration**—By visualizing what you want to do and how you want to react in certain situations, you can prevent your mind from wandering.

2) **Build confidence**—Seeing yourself perform well in your mind makes you feel that you can be successful in any difficult situation.

3) **Control emotional responses**—You can visualize situations that have caused problems in the past and picture yourself dealing with these problems in a positive way. By taking a deep breath and focusing on your breathing, you can begin to focus on the shot to be made.

Courtesy of Rick Sharp

"What other people may find in poetry or in museums, I find in the flight of a good drive.... The white ball soaring up and up into the blue sky, growing smaller and smaller, almost taking off in orbit, then suddenly reaching its apex, curving downward, falling, describing the perfect parabola of a good hit, and finally dropping to the turf to roll some more, the way I planned it."

– Arnold Palmer

4) **Practice your swing**—The best know use of imagery is in practicing your swing or putting stroke. You can mentally practice to fine tune or to correct problems.

5) **Practice course management**—Imagery can be used to plan your course strategy and club selection by visualizing the course and each hole to be played. Imagining the game in your mind will be a mental rehearsal for your real tournament play.

IMAGERY TIP #2

Guideline to Implement Imagery

1) **Proper setting**—It's best to practice in a setting with no distractions. Some golfers like to practice imagery in their rooms before going to sleep the night before a tournament. As you practice regularly, you will be able to use imagery during a competitive game.

2) **Relaxed concentration**—Imagery preceded by relaxation is more effective than imagery alone. Before each imagery practice, relax by using deep breathing, progressive relaxation or self-hypnosis. Relaxation helps you to forget the worries of the day and results in more powerful imagery, as you aren't competing with other events from the day.

3) **Realistic expectations**—Imagery can improve your game if practiced systematically and you are motivated to develop this psychological skill. But results may not come overnight. Dedication to practice will make the difference in the future.

4) **Vivid and controllable images**—Use all of your senses during imagery. Try to feel the temp and sense the movement. Move and position your body as if you were executing the swing, so that the image is vivid for all senses. Work on controlling images so that they produce the desired outcome.

5) **Positive focus**—Focus on successfully completing the desired shot. Use imagery to recognize and analyze errors, as we all make mistakes during play. Be able to leave the bad shots behind and focus on the present. Try to use imagery to prepare for the eventuality of making a bad shot and then successfully cope with the error. Imagine the correct shot an successful execution as well as dealing with negative emotions.

6) **Videotapes**—A videotape of your swing (a picture of your performing your best shot) can provide positive feedback. Observe your swing in a relaxed state and imagine yourself performing successfully each time. Repeat the footage of your perfect swing so that the image becomes imprinted in your mind.

7) **Image execution and outcome**—Imagine the successful outcome of your shot. Be sure to feel the movement and control the image of all your senses. Imagine the feeling of a successful shot.

8) **Image in real time**—If you normally take 20 seconds as a part of your pre-shot routine before putting, then imagine this routine for 20 seconds. If you use the time it actually takes to perform the routine, the transfer to real events will be easier.

Secret 4
Intensity
Regulation

*"I was so nervous out there,
it was pitiful."*

– Tom Lehman

Intensity Regulation

*"To play well on the final holes of a major
championship you have to find a trance and some
kind of self hypnosis that is almost a state of grace."*

– Hale Irwin

*"We all choke, and the man who says he
doesn't choke is lying like hell."*

– Lee Trevino

*"I always envy the man who can miss a shot
and laugh about it—the fellow who takes nei-
ther himself nor his game too seriously. Surely
that is golf seen in its true perspective...It would
help most of us to enjoy the game if we would
adopt that philosophy. But I confess with shame
that I cannot do it. A bad shot, or some silly
mistake at golf makes me fairly boil inside."*

– Bobby Jones

When preparing for an important golf match,
have you ever checked your emotional
intensity level before you set out to play? Do
you feel really energized and ready to play at your optimal
peak performance level? Or do you feel tired and lethargic
and need to "psych up" to meet the demands of the match?

Sports psychologists have found that becoming aware of how much intensity you can handle or even need will allow you to find your optimal performance zone and play at your best. The theory of the inverted "U" by Hanin (1980) (as seen in the chart on the following page) portrays the ideal level of emotional intensity as one in which you are not so relaxed that you lose focus and energy and not so stressed that your performance falls apart.

Intensity can be conceptualized as the energizing function of the mind and body that affects performance. Such things as heart rate, pulse rate, coordination, motor activity, emotional responses and cognitive processes are all a part of the equation. Levels can range from low, as in deep sleep, to high, as in extreme fear. For golfers, intensity can be experienced positively, as increased confidence, motivation, stamina, agility and sensory acuity. Or it can be perceived negatively, as fear, doubt, muscle tension, breathing difficulty, loss of coordination and other debilitating feelings.

When the time arrives for your match, your emotional intensity level will be the most important factor in preparing for your golf performance. There is no one ideal level of intensity for every golfer. Some play best at low intensity; others play better at higher levels. But generally speaking, too much intensity can lead to an over-abundance of stress, which in turn triggers a lack of confidence and a belief that you won't be able to play well. Unfortunately, that belief then all too often becomes a self-fulfilling prophecy. Signs of too much intensity and stress include muscle tension, breathing difficulties, negative self-talk, loss of coordination and the above noted feelings of fear and doubt.

Golfers can also experience under-intensity—times when they aren't stressed enough. If you're overconfident, lack

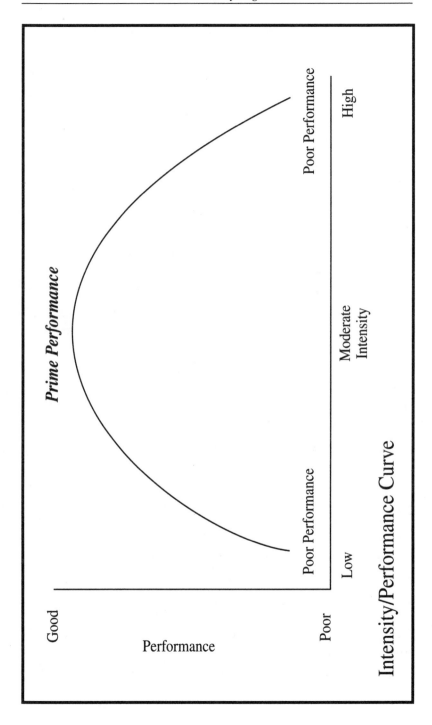

Intensity/Performance Curve

motivation, are tired and/or are not sufficiently challenged, you could be vulnerable for a bout of under-intensity or low performance ability. It may manifest itself as feelings of lethargy and low energy, an absence of alertness/interest and problems with concentration and focused attention, both before and during play.

Most people may realize that they are either "morning" people or "night" people. Having noticed at which times of the day they are most efficient and effective, they'll begin to adjust their productive times to suit their individual style. In the same way, recognizing and regulating your intensity level will significantly improve your golf game. There are several things you can do to check your intensity level and make adjustments so that you are functioning at that peak performance level.

Over-intensity, for example, can be relieved by planning for unexpected events and unfamiliar situations. It can also be controlled physiologically with the use of such proven techniques as relaxation, deep breathing exercises, stretching, progressive muscle relaxation, meditation, self-hypnosis and smiling.

Under-intensity, on the other hand, can be alleviated by "psyching up" through exercises to raise physiological activity, replacing "let-down" thinking with high energy thinking, positive self-talk, and setting challenges for yourself.

Other general techniques to regulate your intensity level include mental imagery, "swing" cues, relaxing music, planning your course management and other pre-game routines you may follow that allow you to become more focused, centered and mentally prepared for your game. Whatever the technique, the goal is the same: You want to keep intensity and stress at the level that helps, not hurts, your game.

How to manage your golf stress

There's no denying that golf is a challenging and sometimes nerve-wracking sport. First tee jitters and/or stress in putting are not uncommon complaints. Few are immune, not even the pros.

Courtesy of Rick Sharp

"Lee Trevino relieves his tension by talking all of the time to other people, to himself, even sometimes in mid-swing. Man how he talks!"

– Jack Nicklaus

Bobby Jones has related how, on the morning of an important match, he would often feel sick to his stomach, his hands would tremble and his muscles felt tight. It seems hard to believe that someone of Jones' stature could get so nervous since he grew up playing competitive golf and was no stranger to pressure-filled situations. He knew what it took to win, and he had what was needed. Stress could have cost him his career, but, through the years, Jones learned how to manage his intensity.

There are many ways you can learn to manage your stress on the golf course. Becoming aware of your own particular style or problem is the first step in the process of making changes to improve your game.

Stay in the present

The anxiety that you feel on the golf course generally starts out at a manageable level—so long as you don't think about it. If you don't think about it, you won't continue to obsess about it and the tension won't rise. Unfortunately, when someone tells you what not to think about, they are giving you the perfect reminder to focus in on it. As you can see, this advice is not helpful and can even make a bad situation worse.

The best thing to do when you start to feel nervous is to distract yourself. When you're thinking about something else, you're not thinking about your nervousness and it doesn't have the chance to build. Golfers have come up with all sorts of ways to distract themselves: singing, whistling, talking to themselves or their partners, telling jokes, taking in the beauty of the course, listening to the birds, recording their score, adding up their putts, daydreaming. With some experimentation, you can find out which works best for you.

Some players have the type of personality that lends itself to distraction. Other players do not. Attempts at distraction don't work, and they're soon back to thinking about their anxiety. If this happens to you, try giving your mind something more important to think about. For example,

Courtesy of Rick Sharp

David Duval has frequently stated that the most important skill he has learned is to stay in the present and play your own game.

before your round begins, you can go to the practice green and become so involved in concentrating on your putting that it's all you can think about. During the round you can focus all of your thoughts on course management and optimal ball position. When you're walking down the fairway, you can recall a great shot that you made in the past when you were in a similar situation.

Thinking about things that are more enjoyable will put you in the frame of mind that will allow you to stay in the present and enjoy the game at hand.

Play your own game

When it's the final round and you're in the lead, there is a tendency to start worrying about losing the tournament. You can become too concerned with protecting your lead. You may start to pay too much attention to the other players, forgetting to focus on your own shots. A roar from a distant gallery unsettles you, because it usually means that someone has made a great shot and picked up a stroke. Most of the pressure is on you. The match is yours to lose. This is not your normal frame of mind, and it's not the frame of mind in which you'll play your best. What happens to many players in this situation is that they stop playing "their" game, neglect to utilize their strengths and start playing tentatively—exactly the opposite of what got them the lead in the first place.

Consider how different it is for the player who's chasing the lead in the final round. When you're moving up the leader board, your thoughts are on winning. You're chasing after the lead, not protecting it. You're not as concerned with the other players. Most of your thoughts are on how to make birdies and eagles. You realize that you have to play your best, and that's what you focus on doing. You feel energized by the challenge. You play decisively. In this frame of mind, there is little time to feel nervous, as more important things require your attention. You know that, if you play "your" game, you have a chance to win.

Courtesy of Rick Sharp

Bernhard Langer has learned that relaxation techniques and a deep spirituality have helped to control the emotional stress and pressures of highly competitive tournament play.

When you're in a pressure situation, playing "your" game is of paramount importance. It will keep you in the right frame of mind and give you the best chance to win. In 1996, Steve Stricker won his first two professional golf tournaments, played on the President's Cup team, represented the United States at the Alfred Dunhill Cup and finished fourth on the PGA money list. Stricker's second win came at the Western Open in Chicago. He was in the lead entering the final round and was playing in front of a home crowd. He was paired with Lee Janzen, who has a reputation for playing well in pressure matches. But Stricker didn't lose sight of what he was there to do. He played his game from the first tee to the eighteenth green. No one even came close to him. After the round, Janzen commented that Stricker played with "zero fear." By playing his own game, Stricker stayed in the moment and emerged a winner.

Common misconceptions about stress

Misconceptions about stress can be as damaging as stress itself and can even increase stress levels. The most common misconception that golfers have about their stress is that it's a sign of weakness. You don't have to look very far to understand why this is such a popular belief. When we read books or got to movies, we are introduced to the hero, portrayed as strong, powerful and fearless. Inevitably, the hero encounters the villain, who is also portrayed as strong, powerful and fearless but somewhat twisted. Finally, there are the victims: powerless, weak and full of fear. Their only hope is that the hero will appear and save them from the villain— which is usually exactly what happens.

This may be the case in books and movies, but when you're on the golf course higher intensity is not a sign of weakness; it's a sign of desire and motivation. It means that you have accepted a challenge and, more than anything, you want to perform at your optimal level. It means that you are willing to deal with stress because you want to win. It is the nature of competition that, at the outset, the result is unknown. If you want to compete, you have to risk, and a higher intensity is part of that risk. The competition can be intense. There can be incredible pressure. It doesn't matter whether it's a five dollar bet, the club championship or the Master's, when you're on the golf course, your intensity arises from your desire to play your best.

If you have the belief that stress is a sign of weakness, then Bobby Jones was a weak person. In truth, Jones is remembered even more for his strength of character than for his accomplishments as a golfer. Jones was challenged by a debilitating muscular disease and responded courageously. He was always comfortable talking about the nervousness he felt on the golf course. Jones understood he felt that way because he liked to compete and wanted to win. Weakness had nothing to do with it.

Some golfers also hold the impossible dream that, if they just try hard enough, they can continually play golf without ever becoming frustrated. It's safe to say that anybody who has this misconception has a terrible memory. No matter how accomplished you are, it's a sure bet that in your golf future you will have many stressful rounds. The most skilled players in the world still top the ball, hook it out of bounds, take two strokes to get out of a bunker and miss 18-inch putts. Golf allows no one to escape occasional frustrations. Believing that you are perfect puts unnecessary pressure and stress on yourself.

If you believe that nervousness is a sign of weakness, you make yourself nervous about being nervous. If you think that you can't play well when you're nervous, you won't. If you demand that you never embarrass yourself, you'll inevitably be disappointed. When you remove these misconceptions from your thinking, you will find that you're staying calm in situations that used to make you stressed.

Managing your frustrations

A close examination of the shaft of Bobby Jones' putter would reveal that it was in less than perfect condition. Jones was fond of his putter and remained loyal to it throughout his career. For the most part, it was a successful relationship between a golfer and his most important club. On occasion, however, Jones would have strong words with his putter and then launch it skyward or slam it to the ground. Because the shaft was made of hickory, it often would be damaged. After a cooling-off period, Jones would make the necessary repairs and the relationship would continue. Jones always wanted to play his best, and when he didn't it upset him, a disappointment borne by his putter. Once, while playing the Open at St. Andrews, Jones became so frustrated that he walked off the course in the middle of his round.

In 1988, Curtis Strange was voted PGA Player of the Year. In 1989, he became the first golfer since Ben Hogan to win the U.S. Open two years in a row. At this point in his career, many considered Strange the best player in the world. But, like Bobby Jones and many other great golfers, when Strange doesn't play well, he becomes frustrated. Early in his career, he didn't always manage his frustration well; by his own description, he was a hothead. However, by the late 1980s, his reputation had changed. As have many champions, Strange learned how to take advantage of his frustration and use it to improve his game.

If you're like most golfers, you've experienced your share of frustration, too. Sooner or later, your performance doesn't measure up to your expectations and you become angry. It's a natural part of the game. But if you want to play your best, you have to know how to manage your frustration so that it doesn't interfere with your performance.

When Bobby Jones acted in a way that was unbecoming for a professional golfer, it was because his frustration was at an unmanageable level. He wasn't able to control it, and it would get the best of him. When you find yourself in similar straits, the first thing you need to do is release some of that frustration. When your frustration is back at a manageable level, it becomes a resource you can channel into your game to help you play better.

When you sense that you're frustration is getting the best of you, take steps to release some of it right away. Having a conversation with yourself may be helpful, or using some positive self-statements to change your attitude will also make a difference. Try to talk things out. If your frustration and intensity are at an extremely high level, you might need to raise your imaginary voice to defuse the situation. Keep in mind that you simply want to release the frustration— never use it to attack yourself.

You also need to remain respectful of the other players and the golf course. By using your imagination to release your frustration, you can maintain that respect. The mind and body are so closely linked that imagining something in your head has nearly the same effect as if you were actually doing it. Have you ever had a pleasant dream and then awakened feeling refreshed and energized? What occurred in your dream seemed so real that you actually felt the benefits. Did you ever wake up in the middle of a nightmare with your heart pounding? The events of the dream were purely imaginary, yet your body responded as if they were actually happening.

Perhaps you're feeling so much frustration that what you really feel like doing is throwing your golf bag on the ground and running the golf cart over it. Ideally, you want to release your anger before it gets to this point. But if your frustration gets to this level, go ahead and act it out in your imagination. In your mind, run over that golf bag as many times as necessary! The important thing is to get your emotions back to a calm and manageable level.

Some golfers try to manage their frustration by holding it inside. This works against the natural physiological tendencies that want to release it. The situation is similar to holding a beach ball under water. It requires a lot of energy and, eventually, it just wears you out. A high price to pay for not dealing with your intensity. Even golfing greats like Arnold Palmer can become frustrated!

Channel your emotions

As a young golfer, Tiger Woods would bang his clubs on the ground after a bad shot. As he matured, instead of taking his frustration out on the equipment, Woods began telling himself, "I'm going to hit the next ball real solid." He learned to channel his frustration back into his game and use it to help him play better. Woods has worked with psychologists since he was eight years old and has learned very early the secrets to successful golf performance.

You can do the same thing. While your emotions are still at a manageable level, think of them as an extra source of energy. You can channel that energy into whatever aspect of your game you wish: to sharpen your concentration, for example, or to increase your determination. If you're feeling tired, use the energy to wake yourself up. If you've started to play tentatively, channel the energy toward playing more aggressively. If your course management has been less than ideal, you can use the energy to help you assess your shots more thoroughly. Decide which area you need to improve and use the energy to make the improvement. If you have some energy left over at the end of the round, go to the practice tee.

Realistic expectations

Your expectations are powerful things, and golfers need to be especially careful about what they expect from their game. Because unrealistic expectations lead to failure and frustration, make sure that your expectations match your level of skill. This will make you a more successful and less frustrated player.

Another reason to be careful with your expectations is that you have only partial control over what happens when you're playing. On a par 3, you may hit a perfect tee shot, only to have a gust of wind push the ball into the water. Instead of a birdie, you're now looking at a bogey or worse. That's frustrating. An approach shot that was right on target takes a bad bounce and ends up in a short-side bunker. Now you need to make a great sand shot to save par. That's frustrating. Your putt is on line with the right amount of speed, but just before it gets to the hole, a divot throws it off course. That's very frustrating and beyond your control.

Any number of things over which you have no control can go wrong. If you always remember that, when you're playing golf, you have only partial control over what happens, you'll be better able to keep unlucky breaks in perspective and continue to play at your best level.

Take a mental break

There are no time outs in golf as there are in other sports. Team players aren't allowed to leave the game until they regain their composure. But while a golfer can't physically leave the course, there is plenty of time between shots to take a mental time out and just use your imagination.

You can imagine that you're at home, sitting in the back-yard with your feet dangling in the pool. Or imagine that you get in your boat, cruising around the lake for a while, and then catch a big fish. Maybe a helpful mental time out for you would be to imagine skiing down a black diamond run in the Rocky Mountains. Perhaps you enjoy listening to music while sitting in your favorite chair. The possibilities are endless. Let's say there is a long delay on the tee of a par 3 hole. You can sit there and stew in your frustration, or you can take an enjoyable mental escape. Mental time outs effectively get your mind off a frustrating situation. When you get back to playing, you'll be calmer and it will be easier to concentrate.

Learning to relax

To improve your mental strength and play better golf, your intensity level can be checked simply by noticing the tension in your grip or the tightness when you swing. Muscle tension can be the greatest deterrent to a smooth relaxed swing like Payne Stewart's. Stewart knew how to relax and let go. He was known for his easy swing and his playful attitude. As Gary Wiren says, "The ability to relax is one of the most valuable tools in the golfer's mental arsenal."

We can all learn relaxation techniques that we can practice at home before a match and utilize when we need them. In the next few pages, you can follow the steps to practice deep relaxation. Or you can buy a relaxation tape (see details on page 192 to order my audiotape, *For Golfers: A Relaxation Hypnosis Program*).

Once you have learned to reach a deep state of relaxation, you can then induce this same state when you use your pre-shot routine to prepare for your shot. You'll find your swing performance will improve.

In summary, if you're like most golfers, you've experienced your share of frustration and intensity problems. The first step in using your emotions to your best advantage is to keep them at a manageable level. When you sense that you are not in control of your anger or frustration, release some of it right away. Try having a conversation with yourself. Give yourself positive affirmations. Try to talk out your anger and frustration.

Use your imagination so that you can remain respectful of the other players and the golf course. Take a mental time out when you need it, imagining yourself in pleasant surroundings away from the pressure of the game. Keep your expectations realistic and practice the following relaxation techniques.

Following this advice will allow you to make the most of your emotional energy, improve your score and enjoy the game as it was meant to be played.

INTENSITY TIP #1

Deep Muscle Relaxation Technique

The following procedure is designed to put you into a state of deep physical and mental relaxation. You can use this procedure the night before a big match to help you stay calm and sleep restfully. You can also use it in the morning to relax yourself.

1) Find a quiet room where you will not be distracted and position yourself comfortably in a chair.

2) Close your eyes.

3) Begin taking slow, deep breaths.

4) Focus all of your attention on your breathing. Let your mind go blank. If thoughts come to you, don't dwell on them.

5) As you continue to take slow deep breaths, begin to relax your body. Start with your feet. Concentrate on relaxing all the muscles in your feet. After your feet feel relaxed, concentrate on relaxing your lower legs. Continue to breathe deeply while you are relaxing your lower legs. Now do the same for your upper legs, buttocks, stomach, chest and back, shoulders, arms, neck and head. Relax each of these areas.

6) In about 15 minutes, you will be in a deep state of physical and mental relaxation.

7) When your mind is in this relaxed state, it is very receptive to suggestions. Before you open your eyes and come out of the relaxed state, give yourself some positive suggestions.

INTENSITY TIP #2

Relaxation Techniques to Use on the Course

Breathing deeply—When on the course and stressed by slow play, a bad shot or distractions of other players, try this quick technique to help you focus back on your game. Simply take the following steps:

1) Inhale slowly, drawing air into your lower abdominal area and then into your chest.

2) As you inhale, imagine all of the tension from your body being drawn into your lungs.

3) Inhale to full capacity, hold for a moment and then exhale slowly. As you exhale, imagine all of the tension being blown out of your lungs.

4) After you have exhaled completely, pause for a moment and focus on the calming effect.

5) Repeat as necessary.

Stretching—When you're nervous, the muscles in your body tense up. You can relieve this tension by stretching. Stretching is also a great way to loosen your muscles before beginning to play a round. Stretch again whenever you feel the tension starting to settle in during the match.

Progressive Muscle Relaxation—You can also loosen up your muscles by systematically tensing or tightening each muscle group for a few seconds and then completely releasing them. You will notice the difference between the tight and relaxed muscle. Doing this will also give you time to refocus your energy and keep your body fine tuned.

Fuller descriptions of these three techniques, along with other home exercises, can be found in the *Relaxation and Stress Reduction Workbook* also included in Appendix A on page 177.

INTENSITY TIP #3
Hypnosis

By working with a professionally certified and licensed hypnotherapist, you can learn this effective technique. Post-hypnotic suggestions can help you make significant changes because they bypass the analytical thinking mind and go straight to the subconscious mind. It has been found that suggestibility increases when you are in a hypnotic state and you are more open to new information and direction. When you can change the way you think, you can change the way you feel and behave. You can begin to eliminate some of the automatic negative self-talk that may be your chief deterrent in mastering the mind game of golf.

I have used hypnosis with many golfers to assist them in changing bad golfing habits. We begin by identifying the habits that are detrimental to their mind game. With positive post-hypnotic suggestions, we have been able to re-direct their faulty thinking patterns and insert more effective ways to achieve positive results in their golfing performance.

After working with a professional to develop this skill, you can begin to practice self-hypnosis on a regular basis to maintain the post-hypnotic suggestions and remain in a relaxed state when you need it in your game. Some tips for the practice of self-hypnosis follow:

1) Find a quiet comfortable private place.

2) Relax any tight muscles. This can be done by tightening the muscle, holding it, then feeling more relaxed as you let go.

3) Take slow, deep breaths. Exhale slowly and gently. Imagine you are exhaling toward a candle so gently that the flame would barely flicker.

4) If you are able to close your eyes safely, do so and recall a safe, relaxing setting, using all your senses to feel as though you are really there.

5) Slowly and soothingly repeat a calming word or phrase, e.g. "I am calm and relaxed" or "I am peaceful and relaxed."

6) If you have goals beyond relaxation, add them to your phrase, e.g. "I am calm and confident;" "I enjoy playing golf, healthy foods;" "I am breathing into my lungs fresh, clean air."

7) Be simple and positive. Do not say "I will not hook my shots." All your unconscious mind hears is "hook my shots."

8) Erase all negative messages.

Meditation—Practicing meditation or yoga techniques at home will also teach you the feeling of being calm, centered and in control of your mind and body.

INTENSITY TIP #4
Keep Things Light

Scientists have recently proven the effectiveness of humor and laughter for decreasing the deleterious effects of disease and illness on our bodies. We have also found that laughter reduces stress. If you enjoy a sense of humor and smile more often, you'll find that it is hard to be tense and smiling at the same time. Let go of tension and enjoy your life.

Courtesy of Rick Sharp

Chi Chi Rodrigez knows how to keep things light—with a good sense of humor—and a smile that helps to keep everything in perspective.

SUMMARY TIPS:

Here are some further tips to enjoy the game and stay relaxed:

1) Smile when you feel tension coming on. Use humor to change your mood and attitude. Keep things in perspective so that you can forget the pressure and enjoy the tournament.

2) Have fun. Enjoy the game. Look forward to pressure situations with a positive attitude and consider the game a challenge to be met. Try to keep "winning" in perspective and focus on the pleasures of the golf game.

3) Set up stressful situations while practicing on the range so that you can become more accustomed to playing under pressure or stress.

4) Slow down your timing and tempo. When anxious, golfers tend to rush their shots. Other golfers may take too much time and their thinking disrupts their swing. Consistent pre-shot routines will help to regulate the pressure and the timing.

5) Stay focused on the present. Thinking about what happened or what might happen usually will increase anxiety. Worries about your score on the previous hole will make you more anxious.

6) Be prepared with a course management plan. Indecisiveness produces anxiety. Making decisions is stressful, so try to pre-plan

7) Keep the game in perspective and enjoy the pleasures it provides.

8) Keep in mind what Walter Hagen has said, "Don't hurry, don't worry. You're only here a short visit, so don't forget to stop and smell the flowers."

Secret 5
Cognitive
Strategies

*"Change your thoughts and you
change your world."*

– Norman Vincent Peale

Cognitive Strategies

*"You must understand that it is your mind that will
have the most to do with how you play
in the big match."*

– Harvey Penick

*"You mind lies at the center of your game because
of its complexity....You need to become more aware
of the role your mind plays in golf."*

– Laura Davies

hat golfers think about and say to themselves
during a match directly affects their feelings,
behaviors and performance. Unfortunately,
what they are all too often saying and thinking causes *poor*
performance. As previously discussed, a golfer's automatic
performance occurs with no conscious thought. However,
the mind can keep up an incredible chatter of thoughts that
have nothing do with the automatic performance. These
inappropriate, misguided or faulty thinking patterns can
create the problems in their game. To improve golfers'
performance we need to address not whether to think but
rather **what**, **when** and **how** to think.

Sport psychology researchers have found that the more
successful athletes use more appropriate thoughts and ex-

pend less negativity and self-doubt. That's certainly true on the golf course. Golfers who have more effective thinking styles are generally more positive and task-focused. Their more positive cognitive patterns seem to facilitate better performance and outcomes.

Distorted thinking patterns, by contrast, can interfere with a golfer's performance by providing the conscious mind with faulty information. Thoughts and attention are often misguided, resulting in emotional distress, anxiety and frustration.

Researchers have found that the more successful golfers employ two common coping strategies: 1) rational thinking and self-talk, and 2) positive attitude and focus. By utilizing

Courtesy of Rick Sharp

Many top players have come to recognize the importance the mind has in the game of golf and have begun to utilize the mental skills they have learned from psychologists.

such interventions as making thoughts more rational, positive and task focused, golfers can enhance their performance.

Irrational thinking

In 1982, Dr. Albert Ellis, a highly regarded cognitive psychologist, identified four general irrational beliefs that may interfere with an athlete's performance: 1) "I must do well in sports, and if I don't I am an incompetent, worthless person;" 2) "I must do well to gain the love and approval of others, and if I don't it's horrible;" 3) "Everyone must treat me with respect and fairness at all times;" and 4) "The conditions of my life must be arranged so I get what I want easily and quickly." These beliefs can create a lot of emotional distress for golfers and contribute to the pressure they place upon themselves to be always successful.

Distorted thinking

In addition to harboring any or all of these irrational beliefs, golfers may employ a number of cognitive distortions that can interfere with their performance. These distorted patterns provide information about the environment that may result in misdirected attention, emotional distress, excessive anxiety or lowered self-concept (Gauron, 1984). A description of some of these distorted thinking styles follows:

1) Perfectionism—Many golfers can get caught up in demanding perfection of themselves in their goals. These unrealistic expectations lead to excessive pressure and undermine effective coping. Perfectionistic attitudes can lead to negative self-concept and fear of failure syndrome due to self-imposed negative consequences when less than perfect performance occurs.

2) Catastrophizing—Some golfers may expect the worst in every situation. Even worse than reality, these expectations can contribute to actual negative outcomes.

3) Self-worth depends on achievement—Many golfers view their value as it relates to their golf performance. This negative self-perception increases pressure to perform better and contributes to low self-worth, both of which can interfere with the enjoyment of the game.

4) Personalization—Golfers sometimes overestimate their personal responsibility for every failure and mistake. This tends to lead to decreased motivation and a lessening or loss of commitment to playing their best game.

5) Blaming—While some golfers over-personalize, others excessively attribute their poor performance to external forces (e.g. the weather, other players, the crowd). Golfers need to be realistic about evaluating their performance outcome and to accept the responsibility to make necessary changes.

6) Generalization—Some golfers will use a single event or incident to define their expectancies for their future performance.

7) Fallacy of fairness—Unfortunately, "fairness" is sometimes mistranslated into wanting one's own way in the game versus someone else's. This perception of unfairness can interfere with the rapport with your golfing partner.

8) Polarized thinking—Sometimes golfers view things in absolute terms and label themselves and others in such one-dimensional terms as "loser," "cheater," "bad opponents." These create expectations that will influence performance.

Self-talk

Self-talk occurs when an individual makes statements to himself, either out loud or in his head. These statements can be judgmental, and golfers can label themselves positively (like an "angel" on their shoulder) or negatively (with debilitating statements spoken only by the "devil" on their other shoulder). Because self-talk serves as a vehicle for making perceptions and beliefs conscious, these emotional and distorted self-statements and personal beliefs can undermine

SELF TALK

What you say to yourself before the shot often determines your success or failure.

golf performance. To put it succinctly, all of the research on self-talk provides conclusive evidence that positive self-talk and self-confidence are directly associated with better performance, while negative self-talk is distracting and can inhibit good performance. Working with a sports psychologist can help you begin to change these statements and affect the thoughts and thinking patterns that influence golf performance.

Improving your self-talk

Golfers can also take steps on their own to improve their self-talk. Bad habits that are "automatic," for example, can often be changed by employing a cue word that serves to refocus attention to the more desirable movement. Just remember to keep the cues positive—remember, the subconscious doesn't hear "not". If a golfer wants to shift weight on the down-swing, an appropriate self-statement would be "shift" rather than "don't hang back." The positive form of this type of self-talk is a good way to correct bad habits that occur automatically. Cue words can also be effective during competitive play. By saying something like "shoot to the target," you can refocus your attention to the task at hand.

Golfers can further use cue word to moderate their physical activity level. Saying or thinking such relaxing cues as "relax;" "slow down;" "go easy" will help you do just that. If your problem is too little energy, try such cues as "get going;" "psych up;" "stay focused." These cue words can be effective in establishing more a optimal level of golf performance.

As previously noted, self-talk can affect your confidence level either positively or negatively as well. Such thoughts as "you're stupid" can harm your self-confidence. It's far better to give yourself a boost—even if you're feeling doubtful—by saying something along the lines of "you can do it!" Minimizing negative self-statements will mobilize a higher level of motivation and yield fewer negative consequences.

You can even use self-talk to help you adhere to your practice and exercise routines. Researchers have found that by using positive self-statements about practice, you can change your attitude, making it far more likely you'll stick with the program of practice goals you have established for yourself.

In order to change your self-talk, you must first become aware of both the content of your self-statements and the frequency of negative self-talk. One easy way of doing so, which I recommend, is to fill your right pocket with golf tees prior to a round. Transfer a golf tee to your left pocket each time a negative thought or self-statement occurs. Golfers have been amazed at the number of tees they have found in their left pockets at the end of play!

Other techniques that can be quite helpful are keeping logs and notes of when self-talk occurs and what it's content is; mentally reviewing holes after play; and trying to be observant of your own mistakes and how they've been affected by your self-talk. Record your thoughts and feeling prior to and during your golf swing. If you are able to watch a videotape of your swing, it can help you with your recall. Trying to become aware of your thinking process throughout your game will allow you to understand yourself better.

Once you have become aware of the content of your self-talk and identified those thoughts that are particularly self-defeating, you can begin to make modifications. You can use any of the following techniques: thought stoppage;

changing negative thoughts to positive thoughts; countering and reframing. (These techniques will be more fully discussed in the following pages.)

A word of caution; however, a golfer must be committed to make a change or modification in his thinking style or these techniques will likely prove to be futile. Even with a commitment to change, without practicing these techniques you will not have success. Working with a sports psychologist can be helpful in identifying any underlying factors that may be contributing to your difficulties.

Thought stoppage

After a golfer has identified his pattern of self-talk that has been problematic, he can begin to eliminate it with a technique called "thought stoppage." This technique utilizes triggers or cues to interrupt unwanted thoughts when they occur. These triggers can be verbal (e.g. saying "stop!"), visual (e.g. a red tape on your club) or physical (e.g. tapping your club on your shoe or snapping the tab on your glove). Any trigger or cue can be used as long as it interrupts the thought and is used consistently. By stopping unwanted self-talk and negative self-statements in their tracks, a golfer can begin to decrease those negative thought patterns and develop a more positive attitude toward his game.

Changing negative thoughts to positive ones

It's not only a good idea for golfers to stop negative thoughts; the ideal is to counter them with positive thoughts that re-direct energy and attention to more appropriate actions that will benefit their game. By substituting a more positive thought, a golfer can negate or at least minimize the effects of the negative thought.

You can begin to implement this technique by making two columns on a piece of paper and listing the negative self-statements along under one of the columns. Opposite each negative statement, write an appropriate positive self-statement that can be immediately substituted the next time the negative one arises.

Once you have come up with the positive statements, you can use them during times of stress on the course. Simply take a deep breath and substitute the positive statements for the negative ones in your mind.

Countering

It can sometimes be difficult to change negative thoughts that are well ingrained into the player's belief system. By using the technique called "countering," the golfer challenges his belief in this negative self-statement.

This process of internal debate—by using facts, reason and rational thinking to counter self-defeating thoughts—can be a powerful tool to stop negative thinking patterns.

Golfers need to develop a case against their negative thoughts in order to begin to destroy the negative beliefs. They need to gather evidence to prove it to themselves. For example, let's say a golfer tends to think, "I get so nervous on the first tee; my heart pounds like crazy. I must be a wimp." He can convert that by rationalizing, "My heart is pounding because this is an important tournament, and I'm very excited about playing."

Reframing

As Norman Vincent Peale has said, "Change your thoughts and you change your world." Using this technique the golfer can begin to change his frame of reference or his view of the world. Golfers may often view the world in narrow, rigid terms. You can change negative self-statements to positive ones by changing your perspective.

Courtesy of Rick Sharp

Amy Benz knows the importance of maintaining a good mental state and positive attitude and how to control both.

For example, you may sometimes say, "I really get embarrassed on the first tee." You can reframe that by saying, "I'm going to see how good I've gotten and where I can improve." Or if your self-statement is, "I'm feeling tense and nervous," you can reframe it with, "I'm excited and ready." Reframing self-statements can help you to keep a proper perspective. If you lose a match, instead of dwelling on the loss you can refocus on it as a learning experience for the matches to come.

A positive attitude

Dr. Patrick Cohn, Sports Psychologist, has said, "Attitude is nothing more than the emotional response you choose to make to happenings and circumstances."

You can't control the weather, the course, the bad breaks or your opponents, but you CAN control your attitude and reaction to them. Golfers like Jack Nicklaus understand that you can't control the outcome of every shot. At the Doral tournament, while needing only a par to win, Nicklaus got an unlucky break when his shot found a large divot hole. His reaction was to survey the situation calmly, select his iron and fire a ball onto the green. He then two-putted to victory. Nicklaus later reported that the bad lie made him focus even more intently. Instead of getting upset over something beyond his control, he chose to control his emotions and maintain a positive attitude.

When you're on the course, you always have a choice. In a tough situation, you can choose to have the mental strength of a Jack Nicklaus and play like a champion—or you can allow your negative emotions to destroy your game.

Remember, your mental state and attitude can affect your performance and you are in control of both. You can choose to stay positive, confident and composed, or you can choose to succumb to fear, anger and the negative emotions that just make things worse. Either way, your score will reflect your choice.

In the accompanying chart, Dr. Cohn, has outlined the difference between a golfer with a positive attitude and belief in himself and one who views himself negatively. With just a glance, you can predict which golfer will be more successful. Becoming aware of your own attitude and making an effort to make a positive change will result in a difference in the outcome of your game.

Faulty thinking patterns

Recognizing the importance of our thinking styles, Dr. Mark Frazier, clinical and golf psychologist, has identified five faulty thinking patterns for golfers to become aware of, which can ruin their golf game. He states, "To play your best golf, your mind has to be working for you. You have to be thinking straight." When you're on the golf course and a faulty thinking pattern develops, you need to identify it and take corrective action, the sooner the better.

Below is a listing of what Dr. Frazier has conceptualized as five faulty thinking patterns that can affect your game:

1) Thinking in extremes
2) Perfectionistic thinking
3) Narrow-minded thinking
4) Self-critical thinking
5) Thinking in the future

Mental Attitude

Great Attitude:

- Views self as a great golfer
- Loves to putt
- Trusts own decisions
- Focuses better with pressure
- Thinks mechanics aren't vital
- Understands one's method
- Can visualize well
- Plays with positive emotions
- Lets it happen
- Simplifies golfing
- Lets go of mistakes
- Practices to make shots

Poor Attitude:

- Views self as a poor golfer
- Fears and hates golfing
- Has low self-confidence
- Changes mind often
- Becomes scared/anxious
- Focuses on mechanics
- Tries to perfect stroke
- Cannot visualize well
- Plays with negative emotions
- Tries too hard
- Makes golfing complex
- Dwells on mistakes
- Practices stroke mechanics

From Dr. Patrick Cohn's book *The Mental Game of Golf.*

These five patterns may seem like a lot to keep track of, but probably only two or three will be relevant to your own golf game. The important thing is to identify which you may be susceptible to and to take the appropriate action to make corrections.

Thinking in extremes

When you think in extremes, everything that happens is either perfect or unacceptable, according to plan or a total disaster, black or white but never gray. Either you drive the ball long and straight every time, or you conclude that you're the world's worst driver. You miss a short putt and say to yourself, "I can never make a putt." Your wedge play is consistent, or you're convinced that you have no short game whatsoever. When the round is over, if you didn't play really well, you leave the course thinking that the day was a failure.

Thinking in extremes results in expectations that are impossible to meet. You put unnecessary pressure on yourself. You become afraid of making mistakes. When you start evaluating your game by extremes, you almost always come up short.

Begin to recognize that you are thinking in exaggerated terms. Tell yourself that what's really going on is that you are frustrated. Take a deep breath and release the emotion.

Perfectionistic thinking

Did you ever stand over a short putt and whisper to yourself, "I absolutely must make this putt!"? With a few holes to play, did you ever check the scorecard and tell yourself, "It's absolutely essential that I finish with pars or birdies"? While preparing to tee off on a difficult driving hole, did you ever say to yourself, "No matter what, I have to get the ball in the fairway"? If these types of self-talk sound familiar, you're involved in perfectionistic thinking.

Narrow-minded thinking

Narrow-minded thinking is like looking at your world through binoculars. A pair of binoculars allows you to view things that are far away as if they were close up. When you look through the wrong end of the binoculars, things that are close up appear to be far away.

Some golfers think with binoculars. When they do something really well, they look at their accomplishment through the wrong end of the binoculars. For example, they finish a round in which they hit nine of the 14 fairways and conclude, "The landing areas must have been really wide." When they do something poorly, they are quick to look at the failure using their binoculars in the proper way. For example, they take no more than two putts on the first 12 greens and then, on the 13th green, they rim their second putt and have to tap in for a bogey. As they walk off the green, they remind themselves, "If I don't start putting well, I won't score well."

When you think with binoculars, you maximize your failures and minimize your success. You take every opportunity to lower your confidence and miss out on the opportunities to build it up.

Self-critical thinking

When your performance begins to fall off and your score begins to rise, it's important to find out what has gone wrong with your game. The key is to look for the fault in your swing mechanics, not in your personality. When you're thinking straight, you can take a critical look at your skills without being critical of your character. You keep in mind that you are assessing things, not your worthiness as a human being. When you become involved in self-critical thinking, you lose this important distinction. You begin to attack yourself with harsh criticisms and belittling accusations.

When you are caught up in self-critical thinking, a double bogey means that you are an inferior person. Selecting the wrong club for a shot means that you are intellectually deficient and have no business being on the golf course. After a couple of poorly hit shots, you turn yourself into a woefully inadequate person who will never measure up.

Self-critical thinking makes it more difficult to get your game back on track. At the very least, it compounds your problems. It's disrespectful to yourself, and it lowers your confidence.

Thinking in the future

When you begin to wander away from the present and start to look ahead, you're guilty of faulty thinking, at least on the golf course. For example you're preparing to putt on the 5th hole, but you're thinking about the difficult pin placement on the 6th green. While waiting to make your approach shot on the 11th hole, you worry about the water that runs along the 12th and 13th fairways.

Very often, when you think in the future, you begin to expect that something bad might happen. Let's say that it's the night before the final round and you have a three-stroke lead. That evening, you let your thoughts run ahead to the next day. You wonder if you will hold up under the pressure of having the lead. You start thinking about the crowd at the first tee, all there to watch you. What if you hit a bad drive? What if you bogey the first two holes? You could really embarrass yourself, if you're not careful.

There are hundreds of ways that thinking in the future can get you into trouble. When you're thinking about what might go wrong the next day, you make yourself nervous for no reason at all.

Tables 1 and 2 provide handy summaries of the five faulty thinking patterns and the results of each. Use them to keep tabs on your thinking, so that you can make corrections as soon as possible.

TABLE 1

THINKING IN EXTREMES—You see things only in extremes of black and white, never gray. Something is either perfect of entirely unacceptable. A great shot means you are an accomplished golfer. A poor shot means you're a hack.

PERFECTIONISTIC THINKING—When you're a perfectionist, you give yourself directives such as you must, you must not, it is absolutely essential, it is entirely necessary. You demand "perfect" results from yourself.

NARROW-MINDED THINKING—When you do something well, you minimize the accomplishment. When you do something poorly, you maximize the failure. Either way, it's a lose-lose situation.

SELF-CRITICAL THINKING—When things are not going well, you look for faults in your personality instead of your swing mechanics. Rather than taking a critical look at your skills, you take a critical look at your character. You begin to make disparaging remarks about yourself and condemn your worthlessness as a person.

THINKING IN THE FUTURE—Instead of staying focused in the present, you allow your thoughts to wander into the future. Most of the time, you anticipate something bad might happen. Instead of playing one shot at a time, your attention is divided. As a result, you do not play your best golf.

TABLE 2

Pattern	Result
Thinking in extremes	Creates impossible expectations
	Promotes frustration
	Adds unnecessary pressure/nervousness
	Increases fear of making mistakes
Perfectionistic thinking	Creates extra emotionality
	Adds unnecessary pressure/nervousness
	Disrupts concentration
Narrow-minded thinking	Maximizes the effects of failure
	Minimizes the effects of success
	Lowers confidence
	Puts you in a lose-lose situation
Self-critical thinking	Distracts you from real problem
	Lowers confidence
	Demoralizes your spirit
	Creates negative self-talk
Thinking in the future	Makes you unnecessarily nervous
	Disrupts concentration
	Loss of sleep
	Creates feelings of anxiety

How to straighten faulty thinking patterns

Dr. Frazier suggest that, once you have identified your faulty thinking pattern(s), the next step is to straighten it out. You want to remove all of the distorted thoughts from your mind. The following examples will illustrate how to do this.

1) **Thinking in extremes**: As you make your way from the 9th hole to the 10th tee, you say to yourself, "That was the worst nine holes of golf ever played in the 20th century. No one has ever played those holes that badly."

   Straighten it out: Acknowledge to yourself that making two consecutive double bogeys has made you very frustrated, but it is not an historical event. Remind yourself not to think in extremes. Tell yourself to direct the energy of your frustrations into sharpening your concentration on the back nine.

2) **Perfectionistic thinking**: You're off to a bad start. When you get to the first par 3, you say to yourself, "No matter what, I absolutely have to birdie this hole."

   Straighten it out: Remind yourself that this way of thinking disrupts your concentration and creates unnecessary pressure. Tell yourself to direct all of your attention to making the best possible tee shot you can. Right now, this is the only shot that matters.

3) **Narrow-minded thinking**: After sinking a difficult 35-foot putt, you remind yourself that every golfer gets lucky now and then.

   Straighten it out: Tell yourself that you took your time and carefully judged the line and speed of the putt. You stroked the ball smoothly, and the results were exactly as you had planned. Don't minimize your successes and maximize your failures.

4) **Self-critical thinking**: You've just tried to go for the green instead of punching out of the trees. Unfortunately, your ball hit a branch and fell into the rough. You immediately start attacking yourself, saying, "How could I be such a moron? I am such an idiot!"

Straighten it out: Remind yourself that you carefully evaluated the risk factors before deciding that it was worth a try. If you had the chance to take the shot over, you would probably punch out. Nevertheless, the outcome of this shot is not a reflection of your intelligence. Remember, if something went wrong with your swing and you want to correct it, you need to look at your mechanics, not your personality.

5) **Thinking in the future**: As you prepare to hit your drive on the 11th tee, you think about how tough the 12th and 13th holes are to play. You tell yourself that it's going to be very difficult to par those holes.

Straighten it out: Give yourself a firm reminder to concentrate completely on the shot at hand. Clear your mind and immerse yourself in the shot. Remember, when you think in the future, you distract yourself.

In summary, the thinking patterns in your mind, like the flight patterns of your golf shots, can also develop a slice or a hook. When this happens, you start to see things in a distorted way. Your mind begins to work against you and golf becomes a very unpleasant experience.

To keep yourself thinking straight, you need to become skilled at recognizing faulty thinking patterns. Once you recognize what's going on, straighten out the distorted thoughts produced as quickly as possible, and you're on your way to being a single digit golfer!

Courtesy of Rick Sharp

Dottie Pepper knows that keeping your thinking straight and recognizing your distorted patterns will help you to be on your way to being a single digit golfer!

Testing Your Golf Personality

Some golf psychologists believe that your personality traits can identify your golfing potential. Dr. Bob Phillips, clinical and golf psychologist, has developed an evaluative behavioral survey that will help you to know how your scores on various traits compare to the desired range of the professional golfer. These reported characteristics are a result of your own self-evaluation. A critical look at your own score will let you know where you could exert more effort to maximize your golf game.

A reproduction of this self-evaluation is located at the back of this book (Appendix B, page 179). See how you rank yourself and note where you can improve.

The traits, which are rated from low to high, include detachment, abstract thinking, emotional stability, optimal arousal, dominance, self-sufficiency, confidence, self-assurance, body tension, tough-mindedness, focus and level of goals.

Your rating on each of these traits will tell you the level at which you're presently functioning. It will provide information about your mental preparation before a competitive event, current level of use of mental game techniques and how similar you are to the more highly successful professional golfers. Understanding your own characteristics can help you to assess your style and to discover which areas may need improvement.

Compare yourself to the 1999 Ryder Cup champions

Having spent time talking with the Ryder Cup American team, it's clear to me that the members understand all or most of these traits. Here are my opinions as to how they would score on Dr. Phillips' survey. See how you stack up against these champions!

- Tiger Woods, a golfing prodigy, would certainly be rated high on confidence, tough-mindedness and self-assurance.

- David Duval, who is very quiet and shy, would be rated high on dominance, detachment and focus.

- Payne Stewart, always the life of the party, would rate high on optimal arousal, self-assurance and goals.

- Steve Pate, a mature, easy-going and friendly personality, used abstract thinking, self-sufficiency and had high goals.

- Justin Leonard, an enthusiastic and high-energy young man, would reflect optimal arousal and self-assurance.

- Davis Love, a "seasoned" and mature player, would be high on detachment, abstract thinking and self-assurance.

- Tom Lehman, a friendly and well liked guy, would be rated well on emotional stability, relaxation and confidence.

- Hal Sutton, always a dominant presence, would rate high on dominance tough-mindedness and goals.

- Jim Furyk, always a nice guy to talk with and be around, is relaxed, focused and has high goals.

- Mark O'Meara, a quiet and very private person, would rate high on self-sufficiency, self-assurance and abstract thinking.

- Phil Michelson, a steady, solid and trustworthy man, is confident, self-sufficient and has great emotional stability.

Check your own personality traits and learn what it takes to be a champion golfer!

Secret 6
The Pre-Shot Routine

"Good golfers use precisely the same
routine for every shot they play."
– Tom Watson, PGA Tour

The Pre-Shot Routine

*"In terms of its influence on the golf swing,
the pre-shot routine is underestimated—
hugely so in my opinion."*

– Ernie Els, PGA Tour

*"If a routine is in my mind, then it occupies my
mind to set-up and hit the shot. It's kind of like a
switch, a mechanism, to get me to concentrate on
that specific shot. If I don't have a routine to focus
on, then, halfway through getting ready to hit the
shot, something may come to mind and I have to
back off and force myself back into that routine."*

– David Edwards, PGA Tour

The purpose of a pre-shot routine is to prepare yourself, as best you can, to make your best shot. The psychological principle behind such a routine is that, by giving your mind exact instructions about what you want to do, success is more certain. Those instructions are given by means of a series of physical and mental steps, each of which is intended to help make the shot the best possible under the circumstances. Almost all elite and professional golfers have a pre-shot routine, because they understand how important it is to the consistency and quality of their play. If a pre-shot routine is not part of your game, now is the time to add one.

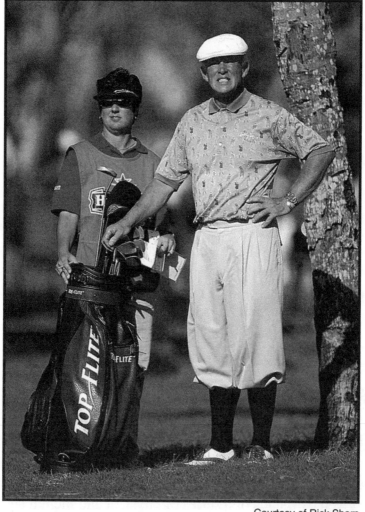

Courtesy of Rick Sharp

Developing a sound pre-shot routine will add more consistency and quality to your game.

Early in his career, Payne Stewart was not aware of the importance of the pre-shot routine. After working with a sports psychologist, however, he developed a sound pre-shot routine. This routine became a solid foundation for his easy relaxed swing, and, using it, he went on to win his major championship victories.

Jack Nicklaus believes that 90% of making a good shot consists of two critical factors: 1) how you prepare your mind, and 2) the consistency of how you set-up to the target. His comment succinctly illustrates both the steps involved in a pre-shot routine and his understanding of the importance of preparation for each golf shot.

Greg Norman utilizes a very exact and deliberate pre-shot routine that is apparent to all who watch him. He visualizes the path of the ball from behind the shot. He walks around the ball, aims his club to the target, aligns his body and sets his grip. He wiggles the club and, finally, moves smoothly into his swing.

Other players, John Daly and Lanny Wadkins, for instance, are more aggressive and take much less time to go through a shorter pre-shot routine. Though different from Norman's, their routines are suited to them and, therefore, effective.

That's one of the keys of a pre-shot routine: it needs to be individualized. While the pros all know the importance of a pre-shot routine, their methods all vary according to their own personal style, the tempo at which they play and what is most comfortable and convenient for each of them. They know a pre-shot routine is something they can consistently count on, regardless of the pressure and stress of competitive play, a "security blanket" that is automatic and allows them to reproduce the same golf shot time after time. With a pre-shot routine, you have a plan of action that allows you to be in the best possible position to be as successful on the course as you are on the practice range.

How to prepare for the golf shot

Developing a pre-shot routine is nothing more than establishing a method of preparation that you use before each and every shot.

As we have discussed, the first important step in preparing for any golf shot is to focus your attention on the shot at hand. No future thinking here; you want to stay in the present and become centered and focused on your plan for this shot. To help you focus, you can begin with a cue or trigger word or action that starts the routine for you (e.g. pulling on a glove, checking your club, examining your ball—whatever works for you to let your mind know it's time to attend to the task at hand).

The next step is to gather the physical information about the shot: the layout of the hole, the direction of the wind, the distance you want to hit the ball and where you want to be to approach the green. Having considered all those, you make a selection of the appropriate club.

A pre-shot routine for putting uses similar steps, but the art of reading the green will be the most important piece of information before you decide on your plan of action. Be sure to check the slope and firmness of the green and judge the distance to the hole and the grain of the green. Select your line and the speed at which to hit the ball.

Dick Hill of the Dick Hill Putting School understands the importance of having a system of preparing for each golf putt. At his own schools, as in his years as head teacher with the David Pelz Putting School, he regularly teaches this routine to his students.

After you assess the variables of the shot and select your club, determine the target and the kind of shot you will want to hit (low, high, fade, draw, etc.). Make a firm decision about

Courtesy of Dick Hill

As the prior head teacher with Dave Pelz, Dick Hill provides a scientific approach to the art of putting which also utilizes the pre-shot routine for consistency and accuracy.

your choice of club and the path and direction of your shot. Never swing the club until you're certain of the shot you want to make. As Harvey Penick says, "Indecision is a killer."

Mentally preparing for the swing

There are a number of mental techniques you can use to help you reach that firm decision with confidence. These techniques employ various senses and functions of the brain. Depending on your personal predisposition, you may find one more helpful than others, but you would be wise to give each of them a try.

1) **Seeing the shot**: Bobby Jones has said, "I have many times holed prodigious putts and chip shots when I felt, before I addressed the ball, that I was going to do so. Often I can see the complete line which my ball must take to the hole. The exact line appears to be drawn out for me."

"Seeing the shot" is a technique in which you stand away from your ball and, in your mind, visualize yourself making the perfect shot. Both Greg Norman and Jack Nicklaus use this kind of imagery as a part of their pre-shot routines. As Norman prepares to make his swing, you can frequently hear his caddy remind to "see the shot." Norman's style is to see the ball as it leaves the club face and starts on its way up. He sees the apex of the flight pattern as a dark circular opening in the sky. Finally, he watches as the ball lands and rolls to a stop, exactly where he wants it to stop.

Jack Nicklaus also sees his shots, but he uses a different method. Nicklaus first sees his ball resting at his target. Next, he sees the flight pattern the ball takes to get there. Finally, he watches himself take his stance and make his swing. According to Nicklaus, when you imagine your shot, you should visualize a "very sharp, in-focus picture."

2) **Feeling the swing**—Ben Hogan has been reported as saying, "I am an advocate of that kind of teaching which stresses the... feel of the movements a player makes to achieve the results he wants."

To imagine "feeling the swing," stand away from the ball and, in your mind, feel yourself making the perfect swing. Alternatively, you can use an imaginary ball and actually swing the club. In both situations, what is most important is that you focus on what the movements of your swing feel like, the actual physical sensation. Having a clear sense of how the perfect swing will feel makes it easier to perform that swing when you're hitting the ball.

3) **Hearing the shot**—Arnold Palmer states, "It's just as important to visualize your putts as it is any other golf shot. Imagine the feel of the putter in your hands, the rhythm of the stroke, the sound of impact; watch in your mind's eye as the ball rolls along the line, takes the break and drops in the cup. I like to think of the ball as sitting on a pair of railroad tracks that run straight into the hole."

While Palmer employs several senses, his advice also incorporates sound or "hearing the shot." To do so, stand away from the ball and, in your mind, hear the sounds of the perfect shot. Listen for the swoosh as the club swings toward the ball. Listen for the click as the clubhead strikes the ball. Hear the ball sizzle as it begins its trajectory. The sounds associated with a well-struck golf ball can be a valuable mental guide when it's time to make your swing.

As part of their pre-shot routines, most professional players will use these imagery techniques each time they make a shot. They do not want to be distracted by anything else and staying with a routine helps them to stay focused. Begin to experiment with your own pre-shot routine until you find what works for you. Maybe, like Norman, you'll be most comfortable relying on the visual. Or maybe, like Palmer, you'll find the most suitable routine is one that incorporates all of the techniques.

4) **Recalling a similar shot**—Greg Norman has said, "If on a certain occasion in my career I was able to slam a one iron 260 yards over water to within a foot of the flag, I have a strong and pleasant mental record of that shot, and when I come to a similar situation it's natural to call on that memory."

This technique differs from the first three in that it involves memory and not imagination. After you have decided on the exact shot you want to play, think back to when you were in a similar situation and hit a great shot. The memory of this shot serves as a guide for the shot at hand. Feelings of success will accompany the memory and boost your confidence. Fred Couples and Greg Norman both use this technique as part of their pre-shot routine.

As you can see, all the professional players have their own personal style of pre-shot routine. What makes them effective is that each is consistent in how he approaches every shot. In other words, the approach becomes "routine." Because it is consistent, it yields consistent results.

The following charts will help you understand the steps of the pre-shot routine. Developed by sports psychologist Patrick Cohn, they list the stages of the pre-shot routine with the corresponding psychological skill that should be incorporated. The examples are for full shot, and putting. (Reprinted by permission from Patrick Cohn in *The Mental Game of Golf: A Guide to Peak Performance*)

A Preshot Routine For Full Shots

Stage of Preshot Routine

- Select a club and type of shot based on specifics of the shot.
- Step behind the ball and select a specific target.
- Align the ball with the target from behind the ball and/or take a practice swing.
- Approach the ball to set up and align.
- Set up and align club and body to the target.
- Make final adjustments, waggle the club and glance at target.

Psychological Skill

- Take time to make sure of your decisions and don't second guess yourself.
- Take a deep breath to adjust level of arousal.
- Imagine the ball flying to the target and identify with the feeling of a perfect shot from the past.
- Reassure yourself that you will hit a good shot–say, "You've hit this shot a thousand times before."
- Focus on the target and/or focus on a swing key such as "smooth tempo."
- Relax and feel the tempo of the swing. Trust you will make a good swing.

A Preshot Routine For Putting

Physical Aspect of Routine

- Standing behind the ball, assess the slope of the green, distance from target, etc.

- Visually engage with the target from behind the ball.

- Approach the ball to set up and take practice strokes.

- Take a practice swing(s) next to the ball.

- Set up and align putter and body to the target.

Corresponding Psychological Skill

- Take a deep breath to adjust level of arousal and plan the shot.

- Create a mental blueprint of the ball rolling along the intended line with the correct speed.

- Use self-talk and cue words to build confidence.

- Physically and mentally rehearse the putt with the tempo that matches the putt.

- Visually engage with line of the putt.

- Release control to your body–trust your stroke.

The importance of the brain

You know by now that the brain is important in the execution of your golf swing, but to understand how much so you need to understand the different functions of the right and left sides of the brain. Although the right and left hemispheres look very similar, neurological research has shown that they are very different with respect to their functions and abilities. These differences lend strong support to the notion that, as the golfer prepares for a shot, there comes a time to "stop thinking and start doing."

Below is a summary chart of brain functions associated with the left and right hemispheres.

Left Hemisphere	Right Hemisphere
Analytic abilities	Performance abilities
Attention to details	Spatial recognition
Mathematical calculations	Perception of feel
Verbal abilities	Non-verbal abilities
Understanding similarities	Recognition of sounds

As suggested by the chart, the abilities of the brain's left hemisphere are remarkably suited to helping you prepare for a shot (thinking). The abilities of the brain's right hemisphere, meanwhile, are especially suited to helping you make the shot (doing).

The left hemisphere of the brain is the analytic hemisphere. The first part of the pre-shot routine, during which you assess the variables and decide on the exact shot you want to play, involves a good bit of mental analysis. The ability to analyze details is helpful as you assess the lie and determine how the weather conditions may affect the shot. Mathematical calculations help you to compute distances. During this part of your routine you should be involved in positive self-talk, using your verbal abilities, also localized in the left hemisphere. In addition, this hemisphere, which is responsible for understanding similarities, helps you recall similar shots from the past.

The right hemisphere of the brain is the performance hemisphere. The abilities of this hemisphere are paramount as you make your swing. A proper golf swing follows a highly specific sequence of movements. You have to get all the right parts, in all the right places, at all the right times. The spatial abilities of the right hemisphere ensure that you make the correct movements. The right hemisphere is also responsible for the perception of feel. As was discussed with regard to the "feeling the shot" technique, your sense of feel can be a useful guide to making the proper swing. The recognition of sounds is also localized to the right hemisphere, and this ability is helpful if you use the technique of hearing the shot.

In short, preparing yourself to make a golf shot is a left hemisphere activity; performing the golf shot is a right hemisphere activity. Once you have assessed the variables and decided on the shot you are going to make, it's time to get out of your left brain and into your right brain. All you have to do is stop thinking and start doing.

This shift from thought to action has been borne out by scientific study. Brain mapping research conducted by Dr. Deb Crews at Arizona State University shows conclusive evidence that, when the elite golfer "pulls the trigger" to start his swing, brain activity diminishes. The golfer relaxes and "lets it happen." As he relaxes, there is no more thinking—the brain quiets down. He simply senses the shot, sees the target, clears his mind and hits!

Mental mapping also helps explain why some golfers are able to repeat their swing consistently. They have developed a well-defined mental map of the exact movements they need to make. This map serves as a guide each time they swing their club. According to scientists, these maps represent actual connections between nerve cells in the brain.

Each time you make a swing, the connections between the nerve cells become stronger, giving better definition to the map and therefore making it easier to follow. But, when you're practicing your swing, it is important that you are careful to make correct swings. If there is a fault in your mechanics, you will develop a mental map for an incorrect swing. By taking care to swing correctly, you reinforce the right way to swing, strengthening your mental map and obtaining consistent results.

At this point in his career, Nick Faldo estimates that he has hit more than 7 million range balls. This amount of practice has likely resulted in a very clearly defined and easy to follow mental map of his golf swing. It would explain, in part, why he is one of the most consistent players on tour as well as the greatest British golfer in modern history.

A positive frame of mind

One final element of the pre-shot routine is to remember to maintain a positive frame of mind. This will allow you to focus freely and without negative thoughts or worries interfering with the routine you've established for yourself.

You can use Sam Snead's technique to prepare yourself before a game and put yourself in a positive frame of mind:

Courtesy of Rick Sharp

Most of the professional players, like Ian Woosnam, incorporate mental skill techniques into their pre-shot routines.

"Whenever I had an important round to play the following day, I would set aside some quiet time the night before to think about what lay ahead. I'd find a comfortable chair in a quiet room and just sit there with my eyes closed, imagining the round I faced. I'd begin on the first tee, visualizing the hole and actually seeing myself play my tee shot, second shot and so on. Naturally, I'd see only good things happening because you must do everything you can to put yourself in the right frame of mind."

By incorporating this type of practice into your pre-shot routine, you can ensure that every part of your mind is primed and ready for play. Then, when you get to the course, you can approach each shot with confidence, knowing you are taking the proper steps to make each of your shots the very best they can be.

PRE-SHOT ROUTINE TIPS:

1) Use your pre-shot routine to help you to concentrate, focus and make the best shot you can. By developing a plan of preparation, you can develop a routine that will get you through any match as a winner.

2) Be sure to remember to see the shot in vivid detail and translate that image into a feeling for the shot. Imagining the shot with all of the senses is the best guarantee of that stroke that feels perfect!

3) At the time of the shot, instead of focusing on the mechanics of the swing, try to allow yourself to feel and sense the shot. This will get you into that zone where it will happen automatically.

4) Your pre-shot routine should have a good pace and tempo. You should not become distracted by negative thoughts or lose focus and concentration, be sure to stop and take a deep breath, re-focus and begin again from the trigger or cue that starts your routine.

5) Utilize the psychological techniques outlined in this chapter to develop your own personal style and create a pre-shot routine that, used consistently, will significantly lower your score.

Secret 7
Golf Goals

"What does it take to be a champion?
Desire, dedication, determination, concentration
and the will to win."

– Patty Berg

Golf Goals

*"All golfers, men and women, professional and
amateur, are united by one thing:
their desire to improve."*

– Judy Rankin

*"No man who golfs is so stubborn, so conceited, so
arrogant or so accomplished that he is not con-
stantly striving to improve his score. He may not
admit this to others. He may pretend that medioc-
rity is enough for him. This man is telling a white
lie and he knows it. He wants desperately to break
90, and, when he does, he will want just as desperately to break 80. Let him shoot in the high 70s,
and he will but one dream: par or better."*

– Sydney James

As the above quotations illustrate, the will to be better
is universal. But if all golfers are driven to lower
their score and improve their game, how do they
find the motivation to realize their desires? One of the best
ways is by setting goals—and don't discount the power of
goal setting. It can get you to where you want to be, and
you'll be thankful for your perseverance and preparation in
the long run.

Most golfers do realize the importance of setting goals to enhance their performance, but before you can establish an effective program of goals, you have to answer some critical questions: How deep is your desire to change your game? What are you willing to do to get where you want to be? And how badly do you want it?

In order to get from just "wishing" and into "action," you will need to follow a goal setting process that is concrete, practical and, most importantly, one that you have made a full commitment to follow faithfully. Goal setting guidelines can be simple to outline, but they are not always easy to adhere to. You need to decide what you want to get from your golf game and then make the commitment to follow through. Write down your goals and plan how you will find the time to pursue them.

Most successful people are well disciplined and focused on their chosen direction. You, too, can become a champion golfer if you will follow the steps to effective goal setting outlined here. It will be your most effective psychological intervention for the improvement of your game.

Steps for effective golf goal setting

Goal setting has been proven both to enhance your performance and to assist with your own growth in the golfing environment. There is, however, no "right" goal program. You need to structure a program that will be effective in meeting your own particular needs. Remember, too, that your success with this process will be directly related to the time and effort that you invest. Give your goal program the commitment and time it deserves and you **will** be able to accomplish your ultimate "dream" goal.

The steps to follow in a goal setting program are:

Step 1: Set specific goals

Set very specific goals that spell out exactly **what**, **when** and **how** you want to accomplish your goals. Be sure they are measurable and framed in behavioral terms so that you know when you have accomplished results and to what degree. It also helps to break goals down into sequential objectives. For example, if your goal is to be able to one-putt every hole consistently, then your objectives would be to consistently make 50%, 75% and 90% of all putts by practicing hitting them from 10, 20 and 30 feet from the hole. Continue to practice until your percentage of successes goes up to a level with which you are satisfied.

Be sure to develop a specific strategy for each objective that you want to accomplish. Keep track of your success with notes and a log book for each day, week and month of practice.

Step 2: Set realistic but challenging goals

An important factor in the attainment of your goals is that they must not only be realistic for you to achieve, but they are also challenging enough to keep you motivated and interested in their pursuit. This is a fine balance. Goals that are too easy lead to less than a maximum effort put forth toward their achievement. You may then be more content with a mediocre performance instead of pushing yourself to your full potential. On the other hand, by setting goals that are too difficult and unrealistic to achieve, you will often set yourself up for failure.

Beware of unrealistic goals that can lead to frustration, lower self-confidence and decreased interest in good performance. A low handicap golfers may have a dream of becoming a professional player—but how realistic are his chances of success? By assessing your abilities clearly and setting goals that, though difficult, are within your reach, you will set yourself up for success, increased self-confidence and better performance all around.

Step 3: Set both long and short term goals

While you will want to set specific short term goals to keep you motivated on a daily basis, you will also want to look at long term goals for the golf season that will keep you focused over time.

Short term goals allow you to focus on smaller increments that are attainable and easier than your "dream" goal. For example, setting daily goals to improve your accuracy in putting percentages is easier to attain than a long term goal to decrease your handicap by six points by the end of the golf season. Long term goals, by contrast, provide a direction and a final result and keep you focused as to where you want to end up.

You can form a helpful mental image of this process if you think of a staircase: Your long term goal is at the top; your present level of performance is at the bottom; and your short term goals are the steps that take you from the bottom to the top of the stairs.

Step 4: Set goals for practice as well as play on the course

Practice goals are as important as competitive and performance goals. Patty Berg has said, "There is nothing in the game of golf that can't be improved—if you practice." The time and investment that you make at the practice tee is directly proportional to the improvements you will make in your game. But only if it is good quality practice that you have organized with a schedule of specific and measurable goals. That will maximize your efforts and allow you to transfer your gains from the practice tee to the course. Your best practice is practice that quickens learning and directly relates to your play on the golf course.

Many amateur players complain that they don't have time to practice and improve their game. Other pressing commitments of work and home interfere with a regular practice schedule. But it's far too easy to find excuses not to practice. Don't let yourself off the hook. Set specific and reasonable practice times, along with written goals that are realistic, and then give the schedule the priority it requires. Doing so will improve the quality of your practice time, and you'll find it to be time well spent.

Step 5: "Ink it, don't think it"

Sport psychologists have emphasized the importance of writing out an action plan of goals to be accomplished with time lines and objectives clearly stated. These goals should always be visible and readily available to the golfer so that he is reminded of his commitment. You can write your goals on 3 X 5 inch cards and keep them in your golf bag. Or you can keep a small notebook in which you record and track your progress toward your goals.

Keeping track of your goals will help to keep your interest high and sustain your persistence. A written record will also give you a sense of accomplishment when you achieve a goal and clearly see how well you you've done.

When writing goals, focus on the positive. For example: write "My goal is to consistently hit the ball on the center of the clubface" rather than "My goal is not to shank any balls today." Record all pertinent data you need to keep track of your progress.

Step 6: Develop goal-achievement strategies

Underlying every successful goal is an effective strategy that was utilized to accomplish it. Without an appropriate strategy to achieve the goal, it remains just a nebulous "wish" with no concrete plan for achievement. It would be like setting out to drive from Pennsylvania to Florida in two days without a road map to guide you.

If you want to learn to hit better bunker shots, you'll have to set up some appropriate learning strategies to achieve that goal: getting lessons from the pro, practicing for an hour three times per week, etc. Once you have identified your strategy and incorporated it into your daily regimen, you have a "map" that will take you where you want to go.

Step 7: Set performance goals

When establishing goals, it's important for golfers to remember to base them on their own level of performance capabilities rather than purely on winning. Often the outcome goal of winning takes precedence over everything, while a game played well may be a more appropriate goal for you.

Ironically, focusing on winning is not the best way to achieve a championship. Sports psychologists have found that too much emphasis on outcome goals (i.e. winning) increases performance anxiety. The consequence is often a poor score. If your goals focus on your own golf performance (how you played), however, you'll be more likely to score better. Doing so allows you to stay in the present and remain focused on the task at hand. As we have seen, staying in the present is one of the ways to make each shot your best shot.

Remember, too, to include enjoyment in your goal program. Researchers have found that by including "fun" as a priority goal, your motivation and persistence will stay higher over the long haul.

Courtesy of Rick Sharp

Practicing your putting with systematic goals in improvement will pay off, as they have done for Aoiki.

Step 8: Goal evaluation

The most important part of any goal-setting program is the evaluation component. Evaluative information and feedback are critical in judging how effective your goals have been toward improving your game.

Periodically planned intervals when time is set aside to look at accomplished goals and review achievements will help you assess whether the goals you set are bringing the results you wanted. You'll also be able to see clearly what remains to be accomplished in order to be more satisfied with your golf performance.

Goals should regularly be re-evaluated and adjusted according to your present motivation level and time commitments. Monitor your improvement with notes and utilize your golf pro or teacher to give you feedback on areas you have been working toward improving.

A sample of the kind of card you can make to track your improvement is provided below.

Goal Evaluation Card: Golf Putting Improvement

Stroke	Specific goal	Strategy	Short-term goal	Target date
Putting	Increase 90% of putts made from 30 feet.	Practice holing four balls each from 10, 20 and 30 feet.	Improve the percentage of successful putts from 50% to 75%	Achieve 75% of putts from 30 feet by end of season

In summary, goals can be an important part of your commitment to lower your golf handicap. Goals can directly affect your golf performance by creating guidelines, increasing effort and persistence and facilitating the development of strategies to improve your game. Goals can also be an influence on your behavior by increasing self-confidence and decreasing anxiety. Maintain your commitment to your goals by rewarding yourself for the goals you have achieved.

Practice goals

Just wishing won't make it so. If you want to make significant changes in your game, you have to practice the goals you've set out to achieve. Having specific goals for practice can help you to focus better on what needs to be improved.

There are two different types of practice goals: 1) physical performance goals that improve the quality of your putting stroke or swing mechanics; and 2) outcome goals, which relate to the quality of the results of your performance.

To help you evaluate your performance goals, ask your pro or teacher to watch your performance and provide feedback. You can also have your swing or stroke videotaped, so you can see exactly how you're doing.

It's easier to evaluate outcome goals than goals used to change your swing technique. Outcome goals. are more specific and noticeable, so you get clean feedback about how you are doing. Using outcome goals helps to keep you involved in practice drills because they maintain your persistence until you attain your goal.

Making practice "real"

To get the most out of practice goals, Nancy Lopez suggests making each shot as realistic as possible. "Instead of just hitting balls," she advises, "make believe every ball rep-

Courtesy of Rick Sharp

Make your practice work more effectively for you by making every shot represent a shot during a round.

resents a shot during the round. Actually visualize the course conditions—where the pin is cut, where the bunkers are, how the match stands."

Golfers often say that they can hit the ball great on the range but can't take their practice game to the golf course. But these golfers often don't practice in a way that makes this transition to the course a simple matter. The anxiety of real play may also interfere in their ability to play as well as they've practiced. The more that you can imitate the situation you encounter on the golf course in your practice, the better the chances are that you'll play to the potential you've set out to achieve in your goal setting.

Many weekend golfers will spend a lot of time on the practice tee, hitting 20 balls in a row with one club, using the same target and making the same shot. Curtis Strange, PGA professional, explains why this technique can be ineffective: "Golf is a target game: you aim for the fairway; then you aim for the green; then you aim for the cup. Yet all too often amateurs hit ball after ball off the practice tee without aiming at anything specific."

Practice hitting different shots at different targets and vary your swing (e.g. hit a full shot, three-quarter shot and a punch shot). The more you vary the conditions of the shots in practice, the more you'll be able to transfer this to the course where you'll have to handle a variety of situations.

Seve Ballesteros, PGA tour professional, has stated, "Practicing out of divots, off hilly or perched lies, off leaves and pine needles, under and over trees, off moist and dry turf and all other goofy situations you invariably encounter in golf, prepares you for both the expected and the unexpected."

Ballesteros finds it helpful to simulate all kinds of conditions on the course so that, when you face them during a match, you'll feel confident because you can recall when you successfully executed that shot during practice.

Courtesy of Rick Sharp

Tom Wargo practices hitting different shots at different targets to vary the conditions and make them more transferable to real situations on the course.

Gradually increase the difficulty of simulation practice by creating challenging scenes. For example, imagine you have a lake in front of you and have to hit over the lake to a small green. Imagine areas on the range that are the boundaries for the fairway. Practice hitting shots with imaginary water on the right and imaginary rough on the left.

Not only should you simulate real and varying conditions in your range practice, you should also incorporate it into your putting practice. This will help develop your feel or touch on the greens and provide experience for different putting encounters you may face on the course. Try practicing a different speed, distance, break, etc. You can better develop your feel by changing the length of every putt you hit. You also need to learn how much a putt is going to break. Practice different drills and from different positions until you gain the confidence you need.

Another good practice goal is to use your pre-shot routine for each full shot and putt. You'll become more comfortable with it and your practice will transfer to the course. You can also mentally practice your pre-shot routine anywhere (office, home, golf course, etc.) or any time as you are using your imagery skill and not a ball.

Practice goals for weaker areas

Nancy Lopez states, "I suppose it's just human nature, but we all have a tendency to practice the things we already do pretty well. In truth, we should do just the opposite if we hope to improve."

So many players make the mistake of practicing shots that they like because they feel good about making them. However, it's more important to work on those goals that will change your weaknesses into areas of proficiency. Be honest about evaluating your game and keep objective measures on your strengths and weaknesses. Make a list of what needs more work and divide your practice time according to what needs the most improvement.

Practice good habits

Ben Hogan has stated, "It really cuts me up to watch some golfer sweating over his shot on the practice tee, throwing away his energy to no constructive purpose, nine times out of ten doing the same thing wrong he did years and years back when he first took up golf... If he stands out there on the practice tee till he's 90, he's not going to improve. He's going to get worse and worse because he's going to get his bad habits more and more deeply ingrained."

Ben Hogan knows that the greatest mistake a golfer can make is to continually practice a bad habit while working toward making a change. The more deeply ingrained your bad habit becomes, the harder it will be to change it to a good technique. Make some assessments of your good and bad habits and make a commitment to seek a golf professional's help with changing a bad habit. All too often we continually practice bad technique and it becomes harder to change.

Goals for mental practice

Your goal program should also include mental practice goals. By practicing your mental techniques, they will become second nature to you and you'll be more easily able to call on them when you need them.

You can begin to practice imagery on the practice range by seeing in your mind's eye the picture of the "perfect" shot. Your goal could be to practice developing the vividness and detail of your imagery pictures and making them as lifelike as possible. The more you use all of your sense in this image, the more clear and vivid it will become.

Another mental goal to practice is developing your ability to feel a solid shot and ingrain the kinesthetic sense for the shots that you practice. You can mentally practice tension control by imagining the pressure you might feel in a tournament and then practice relaxing it away. You can begin to utilize such techniques as deep breathing or tightening and releasing muscles to reduce tension.

You can mentally practice your positive self-talk and affirmations in tough situations by imagining them on the range. You can tell yourself, "I've practiced this shot many times and I'm confident that my swing will be strong and smooth."

Greg Norman suggests, "The tougher the shot I'm facing, the more I talk (to myself). If I'm on the last hole of a tournament, facing a long iron shot to the green and needing a birdie to win, I'll say to myself, 'You know this shot cold, you've knocked it stiff a thousand times and now you're going to do it again.'"

You can use such positive self-statements in your pre-shot routine to help enhance your confidence and help to promote a well ingrained pre-shot routine.

Practicing trust in your swing is very important for optimal performance. You can create a practice drill where you shut down your analytical thinking side of the brain and practice focusing on a target and successfully hitting it. You can continually develop different drills to help build trust in your swing (e.g. practice hitting back off a tee with your eyes closed). Practice hitting balls with good timing and tempo and focus on developing the "touch" for an easy smooth swing. The key is to create drills that can challenge you on each of these techniques.

Practice your concentration skills by focusing on the effort and intensity that is necessary to stay "in the zone" for long periods of time. By staying strongly and clearly focused on the task at hand you will begin to increase your skills of concentration. When you begin to become fatigued on the range and slip out of concentration, focus on key words that will alert you to refocus and become even more immersed in your practice goals.

Practice developing a pre-game routine that will prepare both your mind and body for the tournament. Amy Alcott has a routine she always follows before teeing off, and it has helped her to win 32 tournaments. She gets to the course 45 minutes before tee time and begins to stretch her muscles. She then warms-up by hitting a few wedge shots and visualizes each one. She uses every club but does not leave a club until she has hit solidly. She finishes with a wedge to develop timing and tempo. She then hits a few putts and chips to develop her touch. It seems to be a good systematic routine that works for her and prepares her mentally for her game by putting her in the right frame of mind with a winning and confident attitude. The important key is that she does not rush herself out to the first tee.

Instead, she takes the time to utilize the routine that puts her mind in the best mental condition to perform at her peak performance level.

Physical preparation for the game

Now that you've learned all of the mental skills to prepare for your best round of golf, it's time to mention the physical side of things. Although your mind is vitally important in the game, golf does obviously involve physical effort too. Therefore, you'll want to take care of your body with warm-up exercises to loosen and stretch your muscles so that they won't be tight during play. There are many good stretching routines to follow. Practice the one that works best to loosen <u>you</u> up and gets you ready to play.

Warming-up with your practice swings on the range is an important routine that will get you ready for the course. Getting the feel of your swing and practicing focused concentration will prepare you for an exciting match. With body and mind relaxed and working together, you'll be ready to play golf the way it was meant to be played!

In summary, using the goal setting process, outlined herein, will provide a framework for you to begin the changes in your game in which you've decided to invest your time and effort.

Your pay-off is reflected in the following photo of Helen Alfredson, you'll enjoy the game as much as she does!

Courtesy of Rick Sharp

Helen Alfredson reflects the joy that a good golf game can bring!

Conclusion

"One of the most fascinating things about golf is how it reflects the cycle of life. No matter what you shoot, the next day you have to go to the first tee and begin all over again and make yourself into something."

– Peter Jacobsen

As the above quotation so wonderfully puts it, the game of golf is very much like life itself. Your successes in both depend largely upon your attitude, perspective, self-discipline and perseverance. Yes, natural talent plays a role. But such talent is only good as far as you use it. If you don't work it, if you don't continually strive to better yourself, your talent just lies fallow.

In golf and in life, you need to apply yourself. And you need to pay attention to what's going on in your mind—your thoughts, your self-talk, your tough-mindedness—or you're apt to end up somewhere you didn't expect and don't want to be.

I mention these parallels between the game of golf and life because, as a psychologist, I've seen how the same negative patterns can harm performance in all arenas, be it sports, work or personal relationships. I've also seen how positive attitudes and thoughts can help someone surmount seemingly impossible obstacles and achieve fantastic goals.

The same psychological principles I've detailed in this book—as they relate to better golf—are just as applicable to other areas of your life. In my practice, I've worked with golfers, consulted with businesses and counseled individuals. In every case, we begin by identifying problems; then we implement the best tactics to right them. By and large, those tactics are what I've here termed the 7 Secrets to *Master the Mind Game of Golf.*

Consider, for example, that those golfers who do the best, who make it to the top, are those who have a great attitude toward both the sport and their own performance and who have the determination to persevere in their quest to be the best. Tiger Woods didn't just burst into the top ranks of professional golfers. He's worked toward that goal almost all of his life. Remove the word "golf" and the same can be said about Bill Gates or Jackie Joyner Kersee or Albert Einstein or any of the others whom the world considers outstanding successes. All of these people understood that achieving great results requires hard work—but work that can be incredibly enjoyable. This is the essence of *real* talent.

Real talent doesn't mean you don't ever fail. Lots of great men and women have experienced numerous failures. What made them great, however, was that they recognized these were just way stations on the road to success. They learned from their failures and ultimately succeeded on a grand scale. Their success came not because they were "better people," but because they were committed to their goals, believed they could achieve them and never stopped working or loving their work.

Your dreams and goals—whether on the golf course or in other areas of your life—may be grand or modest. Regardless of their size and scope, you can help yourself achieve them by implementing the principles and techniques in this book. There are also a few other things to "keep in mind" that will help you on your way to success.

Attitude is everything. By viewing stress or failure as challenges to overcome, you conquer the urge to see them as something to fear and run away from. All it takes is a change in perspective.

"Life, like golf, can be humbling," says Grantland Rice, sportswriter and a good friend of Bobby Jones. "However, little good comes from brooding about mistakes we've made. The next shot, in golf or in life, is the big one."

By maintaining that kind of perspective, you will be well on your way toward overcoming the obstacles placed in your path. There's nothing wrong with being humble—or humbled—as long as it doesn't stop you in your tracks.

The importance of role models cannot be overstated. Remember that about half of all learning derives from modeling. So if you want to be a better golfer, watch the pros. If you want to succeed in business, find out how others have done so. If you want to be a better parent, notice how parents you admire do the job.

In a similar vein, remember to surround yourself with people who share your positive attitude and who are supportive of your endeavors. They are the ones who will spur you to further heights—and who will be there when you need propping up. Stay away from people whose negative or angry attitudes bring you down. If you're playing golf, you want to do it with partners who enjoy the game as much as you do and who not only believe you can make that birdie but who will celebrate with you when you do.

That's not always possible, of course. If you're involved in a highly competitive playoff match, chances are your opponent won't exactly cheer if you do well. The same is true if you're bidding against another businessman for a lucrative contract. But by bringing as many positive people into your life as you can, you lay indelible foundations of support— much like the mental mapping of your golf swing—that can help to keep your confidence high even in times of stress.

And don't forget to smile. That may be the best advice of all. Smiling reduces tension, but it also reminds you of why you started playing golf in the first place—for the enjoyment of the game. The same, needless to say, is true of any endeavor in life.

In my seminars, I usually close by telling those assembled that there is an art to golf that is equally applicable to life. The lessons learned on the course can be transferred to so many of our daily activities. Golf teaches myriad things relevant to life, from living in the present moment to learning to trust and accept ourselves. If you take advantage of the education it offers, you will not only experience the joy of golf, but you'll also experience the joy of life.

Nearly everything I have laid out in this book can be applied throughout your life as well as to improve your golf performance. Let me leave you with these words from Arnold Palmer:

"Golf satisfies the soul and frustrates the intellect.
It is at the same time rewarding and maddening—
and it is without doubt the greatest game mankind
had ever invented."

I hope you'll employ these "secrets" to achieve better golf—and a great life!

𝕬𝕡𝕡𝕖𝕟𝕕𝕚𝕩 𝕬

Additional Relaxation Techniques from
The Relaxation and Stress Reduction Workbook

Breathing Awareness

1. Lie down on a rug or blanket on the floor in a "dead body" pose—your legs straight, slightly apart, your toes pointed comfortably outwards, your arms at your sides, not touching your body, your palms up, and your eyes closed.

2. Bring your attention to your breathing, and place your hand on the spot that seems to rise and fall the most as you inhale and exhale. Note that if this spot is in your chest, you are not making good use of the lower part of your lungs. People who are nervous tend to breathe many short, shallow breaths in their upper chest.

3. Place both of your hands gently on your abdomen and follow your breathing. Notice how your abdomen rises with each inhalation and falls with each exhalation.

4. It is best if you breathe through your nose. If possible, clear your nasal passages before doing breathing exercises.

5. Is your chest moving in harmony with your abdomen, or is it rigid? Spend a minute or two letting your chest follow the movement of your abdomen.

6. Scan your body for tension, especially your throat, chest and abdomen.

Deep Breathing

1. Although this exercise can be practiced in a variety of poses, the following is recommended: lie down on a blanket or rug on the floor. Bend your knees and move your feet about eight inches apart, with your toes turned outward slightly. Make sure your spine is straight.

2. Scan your body for tension.

3. Place one hand on your abdomen and one hand on your chest.

4. Inhale slowly and deeply through your nose into your abdomen to push up your hand as much as feels comfortable. Your chest should move only a little and only with your abdomen.

5. When you feel at ease with step 4, smile slightly, inhale through your nose and exhale through your mouth, making a quiet, relaxing, whooshing sound like the wind as you blow gently out. Your mouth, tongue and jaw will be relaxed. Take long, slow, deep breaths which raise and lower your abdomen. Focus on the sound and feeling of breathing as you become more and more relaxed.

6. Continue deep breathing for about five or ten minutes at a time, once or twice a day, for a couple of weeks. Then if you like, extend this period to 20 minutes.

7. At the end of each deep breathing session, take a little time to once more scan your body for tension. Compare the tension you feel at the conclusion of the exercise with that which you experienced when you began.

8. When you become at ease with breathing into your abdomen, practice it whenever you feel like it during the day when you are sitting or standing. Concentrate on your abdomen moving up and down, the air moving in and out of your lungs, and the feeling of relaxation that deep breathing gives you.

9. When you have learned to relax yourself using deep breathing, practice it whenever you feel yourself getting tense.

The Relaxing Sigh

During the day you probably catch yourself sighing or yawning. This is generally a sign that you are not getting enough oxygen. Sighing and yawning are your body's way of remedying the situation. A sigh is often accompanied by a sense that things are not quite as they should be and a feeling of tension. A sigh releases a bit of tension and can be practiced at will as a means of relaxing.

1. Sit or stand up straight.

2. Sigh deeply, letting out a sound of deep relief as the air rushes out of your lungs.

3. Don't think about inhaling—just let the air come in naturally.

4. Repeat this procedure eight to twelve times whenever you feel the need for it, and experience the feeling of relaxation.

Appendix B

Personality Characteristics Behaviorial Survey from the Golf Psychology Training Center

Evaluation Feedback of Personality Characteristics and Behavioral Survey.

Your personality trait scores are compared to the personality traits of highly successful professional golfers. These traits have been found to differentiate between professional golfers and highly successful professional golfers. Compare your scores with the desired ranges in most topic areas below. Behavioral characteristics reflect your self-reported score and what level of effort I think you need to exert in that area to maximize your golf.

Detached (Warmth)

Your ability to separate yourself from people and circumstances during competition, becoming more internally focused.

Desired level 3 to 4   Your score _____.

I am able to separate myself from other players and situations during competition.

Score: ____   Amount of work needed in this area: **High   Med.   Low**

I am able to focus on what is important and not be distracted by thoughts, other golfers or unimportant events.

Score: ____   Amount of work needed in this area: **High   Med.   Low**

Other golfers see me as getting more centered on my game as the pressure increases.

Score: ____   Amount of work needed in this area: **High   Med.   Low**

Abstract Thinking (Reasoning)

Your ability to use your intellect to your advantage rather than your disadvantage while playing in a competitive round. Being creative in planning and completing your shot.

Desired level 6 to 7   Your score _____.

Behavioral aspects of abstract thinking.

I develop a strong game-plan for managing the course, deciding on clubs, targets, and types of shots prior to the start of the tournament.

Your score: ____   Amount of work needed in this area: **High   Med.   Low**

179

I commit to a game plan that maximizes my current skills on "this" course even if it differs from what others think I should do.

Your score: _____   Amount of work needed in this area: **High   Med.   Low**

I resist getting too abstract, over-analyzing shots or greens.

Your score: _____   Amount of work needed in this area: **High   Med.   Low**

I avoid getting technical and/or mechanical during pre-tournament round practice, I prefer to get loose, work on tempo, speed of play and feeling confident.

Your score: _____   Amount of work needed in this area: **High   Med.   Low**

I focus on swing-thought for the day and developing my pre-shot routine during my pre-round warm-up.

Your score: _____   Amount of work needed in this area: **High   Med.   Low**

After a bad shot or putt, I check my tempo and pre-shot routine before I analyze my physical flaws.

Your score: _____   Amount of work needed in this area: **High   Med.   Low**

After a bad shot or putt, I have a preplanned way of leaving the negative emotions behind me so that I do not take them to the next shot or putt.

Your score: _____   Amount of work needed in this area: **High   Med.   Low**

Emotional Stability

Your ability to minimize your emotional reactions to everything, good or bad, including: your shots, your lies, your luck, the conditions, the marshals, any pain, media and other people.

Desired level 6.5 to 7.5   Your score _____.

I can usually accept a poorly executed shot or putt before hitting my next shot or putt. I let it go quickly.

Your score: _____   Amount of work needed in this area: **High   Med.   Low**

It is possible for me to follow-up a really bad hole or round, with a really good hole or round.

Your score: _____   Amount of work needed in this area: **High   Med.   Low**

It is fairly difficult for someone watching my play and external emotions to determine my level of play during competition.

Your score: _____   Amount of work needed in this area: **High   Med.   Low**

My caddie would say I remain composed even on difficult days.

Your score: _____   Amount of work needed in this area: **High   Med.   Low**

Optimal Arousal

Your ability to maintain the optimal level of emotional (not physical) tension. An arousal level that is either too high or too low will result in reduced performance.

I am generally "psyched up" or aroused enough by competition to feel motivated and excited about tournament play.

Your score: _____   Amount of work needed in this area: **High   Med.   Low**

I can manage my focus during competition so that my attention seldom drifts aimlessly (because of being too relaxed or under-aroused).

Your score: _____   Amount of work needed in this area: **High   Med.   Low**

I can manage my focus during competition in such a way that it seldom jumps rapidly to irrelevant variables during execution of shots and putts (because of being too tense or over-aroused.

Your score: _____   Amount of work needed in this area: **High   Med.   Low**

I can generally intercept and change my thoughts when expectations and "outcome thinking" (i.e. thinking of the score, money, place on leader board, etc.) make me too tense (over-aroused) to swing naturally.

Your score: _____   Amount of work needed in this area: **High   Med.   Low**

Dominance

Your ability to consistently approach the current round with a strong, but not extreme, level of aggressiveness; one that will allow you to challenge the course.

Desired level 6 to 7   Your score _____.

I take a moderately aggressive approach to course management, creating (not just waiting) for opportunities.

Your score: ____   Amount of work needed in this area: **High**   **Med.**   **Low**

When considering a difficult shot, I believe that I have greater than a 50% chance of making it before committing.

Your score: ____   Amount of work needed in this area: **High**   **Med.**   **Low**

I stay with my game-plan, resisting getting "careful" or "protective" when I am having a very good round.

Your score: ____   Amount of work needed in this area: **High**   **Med.**   **Low**

I stay with my game-plan, resisting getting more aggressive and taking forceful, high risk shots when having a very good round.

Your score: ____   Amount of work needed in this area: **High**   **Med.**   **Low**

I stay with my game-plan, resisting aggressive, forceful, high risk shots to make up for lost strokes.

Your score: ____   Amount of work needed in this area: **High**   **Med.**   **Low**

Self-sufficient (Self-reliance)

Your ability to not only make your own decisions, but your preference for doing so.

Desired level 7 to 8   Your score _____.

I prefer to make my own decisions and not rely on the advise of others.

Score: ____   Amount of work needed in this area: **High**   **Med.**   **Low**

Making decisions as to club selection, swing, and target are easy and natural for me.

Score: _____   Amount of work needed in this area: **High   Med.   Low**

I am completely committed to the club, swing and target before I swing.

Score: _____   Amount of work needed in this area: **High   Med.   Low**

Confidence

Confidence is about how you feel about yourself and how you feel about your abilities. Confidence is about your attitude and your expectations

I believe I have the ability to achieve my goals as a competitive golfer.

Your score: _____   Amount of work needed in this area: **High   Med.   Low**

Most of my imagery prior to a competitive round is of what "good" can happen as opposed to what "bad" can happen.

Your score: _____   Amount of work needed in this area: **High   Med.   Low**

My "self-talk", both aloud and to myself. during a competitive round is positive, constructive and supportive rather than negative, destructive and discouraging.

Your score: _____   Amount of work needed in this area: **High   Med.   Low**

It is unusual for me to experience extreme fear over a shot or putt.

Your score: _____   Amount of work needed in this area: **High   Med.   Low**

Self-assured (Apprehension)

Your ability to really like yourself no matter how well, or how poorly, you are playing.

Desired level 3 to 4   Your score _____.

I truly like myself, even when I play poorly.

Score: _____   Amount of work needed in this area: **High   Med.   Low**

I do not feel guilty or ashamed of myself when I play poorly.

Score: _____   Amount of work needed in this area: **High   Med.   Low**

I tend to be supportive of my learning and I feel generally confident of final success.

Score: _____   Amount of work needed in this area: **High   Med.   Low**

Relaxed (Body Tension)

Your ability to maintain the proper level of physical arousal for competition.

Desired level 5 to 6   Your score _____.

I periodically check my body for tension during a round.

Score: _____   Amount of work needed in this area: **High   Med.   Low**

I have a specific way of dealing with body tension when I am on the course.

Score: _____   Amount of work needed in this area: **High   Med.   Low**

I can compete without my body tensing up, especially my hands and shoulders.

Score: _____   Amount of work needed in this area: **High   Med.   Low**

Tough Minded

Your ability to maintain a strong self-reliant, non-sensitive, realistic and rational attitude during competition.

Desired level 7 to 8   Your score _____.

I persist and resist giving up or "quitting" under even the most adverse circumstances.

Your score: _____   Amount of work needed in this area: **High   Med.   Low**

1 can effectively resist being sensitive to and affected by the gamesmanship of others.

Your score: _____   Amount of work needed in this area: **High   Med.   Low**

During competition I can detach emotionally from a playing partners bad round. even if we are good friends.

Your score: _____   Amount of work needed in this area: **High   Med.   Low**

I can compete without being distracted by sensitivities toward the thoughts, concerns, or opinions of others.

Your score: _____   Amount of work needed in this area: **High   Med.   Low**

Focus

Your ability to be in the optimal mental position and to flow mentally from one position to the next. Your ability to be in the optimal time frame (past, present and future) to enhance your ability to play your best golf.

I use a strong mental routine, in addition to my physical routine for almost all of my shots and putts.

Your score: _____   Amount of work needed in this area: **High   Med.   Low**

I effectively commit to each club, target and shot before stepping up to the ball.

Your score: _____   Amount of work needed in this area: **High   Med.   Low**

I effectively visualize each shot or putt before I step up to the ball.

Your score: _____   Amount of work needed in this area: **High   Med.   Low**

I am not distracted by my own thoughts during play.

Your score: _____   Amount of work needed in this area: **High   Med.   Low**

I am not distracted by external events, sounds or other distractions during play.

Your score: _____   Amount of work needed in this area: **High   Med.   Low**

I stay with my mental routine even when it is toughest to do so (i.e. when in contention, or even the lead, or when struggling with the physical game.)

Your score: _____   Amount of work needed in this area: **High   Med.   Low**

Goals

Motivation, planning, expectation and results are all governed by your goals.

I have specific and personal goals concerning my golf game.

Your score: _____   Amount of work needed in this area: **High   Med.   Low**

I have specific mental training goals for each practice round I play.

Your score: _____   Amount of work needed in this area: **High   Med.   Low**

I am emotionally prepared to do what is necessary to reach my golf goals.

Your score: _____   Amount of work needed in this area: **High   Med.   Low**

I am in touch with how it will feel to be very successful in golf.

Your score: _____   Amount of work needed in this area: **High   Med.   Low**

General Results

These general ratings rate your current level of use of the various mental game techniques. I have used a one (low) to ten (high) ratting.

Level of mental preparation before each competitive event. _____

Level of current use of the mental game techniques. _____

Level of similarity with highly successful professional golfers. _____

Areas of current strengths in the mental game:

1. _____

2. _____

3. _____

Recommended areas of concentration for the first month of training:

1. _____

2. _____

Bibliography and Suggested Reading

Alcott, A. and Wade D. (1991) *Amy Alcott's Guide to Women's Golf* — Penguin Books USA, Inc., New York, New York

Ballesteros, S. and Andrisani, J. (1988) *Natural Golf*—McMillan Publishing, New York

Brown, R. (1994)—*The Golfing Mind: The Psychological Principles of Good Golf.* Lyons and Buford, Publishers: New York

Cohn, P. J. (1994)—*The Mental Game of Golf: A Guide to Peak Performance.* Diamond Communications, Inc., South Bend, Indiana

Cohn, J. P. and Winters, R. K. (1995)—*The Mental Art of Putting.* Diamond Communications, Inc., South Bend, Indiana

Cohn, P., Rotella, R. and Lloyd, J. Effects of a Cognitive-Behavioral Intervention on the Pre Shot Routine and Performance in Golf. *The Sport Psychologist,* 1990. 4, 33-47.

Coop, R. H. (1993)—*Mind Over Golf.* Macmillan: New York

Crews, D. J. and Landers, D. M. (1993) Electroencephalographic Measures of Attention Patterns prior to the golf putt. *Medicine and Science in Sports and Exercise,* 25 (1), 116 - 126.

Crews, D., McCormick, S. Lochbaum, M. and Lutz, R. *A Comparison of Three Psychological Training Techniques on Golf Performance* (unpublished manuscript).

Davis, M., Eshelman, E. and McKay, M. (1988) *The Relaxation and Stress Reduction Workbook.* New Harbinger Publications, 5674 Shahuck Avenue, Oakland, CA 94609

Ellis, A. (1982) *Rational Living*—self-direction in sport and life. A. E. and Harper, R.A. (1975). A new guide to rational living. Prentice-Hall, Englewood Cliffs, New Jersey.

Frazier, M. (1995) *The Six Mental Fundamentals of Golf* — (unpublished manuscript)

Gallwey, T. (1979)—*The Inner Game of Golf.* Random House: New York, New York

Gauron E. F. (1984) *Mental Training for Peak Performance*—Sport Science Associates, Lansing, New York.

Golfers On Golf: Witty, Colorful and Profound Quotations on the Game of Golf (1997). Selected and edited by Downs, Mac Rury. R. R. Donnelley and Sons Company, General Publishing Group, Los Angeles, California

Gould, D. (1992) *Applied Sport Psychology: Personal Growth to Peak Performance*—Goal Setting for Peak Performance. In J. Williams (Ed.) (2nd ed.) (pp 158 - 169). Mayfield, Mountain View, California

Graham, D. (1990)—*Mental Toughness Training for Golf*, Pelham Books: New York, New York

Hanen, Y. L. (1980) Sports Psychology: *An Analysis of Athlete Behavior*— A study of anxiety in sports. In W. F. Straub (Ed.) (pp 236 - 249). Ithaen, New York: Mouvement.

Harris, D. V. (1986) *Personal Growth to Peak Performance*— Relaxation and Energizing Techniques for Regulation of Arousal. In J. M. Williams (Ed.) (pp 185 - 207). Mayfield, Palo Alto, California

Heyman, S. R. (1984) *Cognitive Interventions: Theories, Applications and Cautions.* In W. F. Straub & J. M. Williams (Eds.) Cognitive Sport Psychology. Sport Science Associates, Lansing, NY pp 289-303

Hogan, C. (1993)—*Learning Golf.* Sports Enhancement Associates, Inc., Zediker Publishing: Clifton, Colorado

Horn, T. S. (Ed.) (1992)—*Advances in Sports Psychology.* Human Kinetics Publishers, Inc.: Champaign, Illinois

Jackson, A. (1989)—*Stress Control Through Self-Hypnosis.* Double Day, Sydney, Australia.

Jackson, A. (1995) *Eye on the Ball Mind on the Game: An Easy Guide to Stress-Free Golf*, Barnes and Noble Books, New York, New York.

Kite, T. and Dennis L. (1990)—*How to Play Consistent Golf.* Golf Digest/Tennis, Inc., Trumbull, Connecticut

Lopez, N. and Wade, D. (1987)—*Nancy Lopez's The Complete Golfer.* Contemporary Book, Chicago, Illinois

MacKenzie, Marlin M. (1990)—*Golf the Mind Game.* Dell Publishing: New York, New York

Miller, Larry (1986)—*Beyond Golf.* Stillpoint Publishing: Walpole, New Hampshire

Nicklaus, J. and Bowden, K. (1974)—*Golf My Way.* Simon and Schuster: New York, New York

Norman, G. and Peper, G. (1993)—*Greg Norman's Instant Lessons.* Simon & Schuster, New York, New York

Owens, D. D. and Kirschenbaum, D. (1998)—*Smart Golf.* Jossey-Bass, Inc., Publishers, San Francisco, California

Palank E. (1999) *The Golf Doc: Health, Humor and Insight to Improve Your Game*—Jones and Bartlett, Boston, Massachusetts

Penick, H. and Shrake, B. (1992) *Harvey Penick's Little Red Book*—Simon and Schuster: New York, New York

Rotella, B. (1995)—*Golf is Not a Game of Perfect.* Simon and Schuster: New York, New York

Rotella, B. (1996)—*Golf is a Game of Confidence.* Simon and Schuster: New York, New York

Rotella, B. (1999)—*Life is Not a Game of Perfect.* Simon and Schuster: New York, New York

Shapiro, A. (1996)—*Golf's Mental Hazards.* Simon and Schuster: New York, New York

Sheehan, E. (1995)—*Self-Hypnosis: Effective Techniques for Everyday Problems*—Element Books Limited. Rockport, Massachusetts

Shoemaker, F. (1996)—*Extraordinary Golf.* G. P. Putnam and Sons: New York, New York

VanRaalte, J. L. and Brewer, B. W. (1996)—*Exploring Sport and Exercise Psychology.* American Psychological Association: Washington, D.C.

Varcoe, M. (1997) *For Golfers: A Relaxation Hypnosis Program.* A relaxation audio-cassette.

Weinberg, R. S. (1992). Goalsetting and Motor Performance: A Review and Critique. In G. C. Roberts (Ed.) *Motivation in Sport and Exercise* (pp 177 - 198). Human Kinetics, Champaign, Illinois

Wiren, Gary (1999). *The Golf Magazine Mental Golf Handbook.* The Lyons Press, New York, New York 10011

About the Author

❧❀❧

Dr. Marilyn J. Varcoe, psychologist, educator, lecturer, author, and founder of Golf Smart™, Inc., has worked with individuals; has provided numerous programs and seminars to businesses and corporations; and has made frequent television appearances, including *The Golf Channel*. She has written articles for regional magazines including *Golf Coasting* magazine.

Dr. Varcoe has taught classes at the university level, and maintained a private practice for 20 years in Pennsylvania and Florida. She obtained her Ph.D. in Counseling Psychology from Pennsylvania State University and her Master's degree from Southern Illinois University.

To Contact the Author:

Dr. Marilyn J. Varcoe
Golf Smart, Inc.

P O Box 770412, Naples, FL 34107-0412
941-514-3015 • 888-404-9682 • Fax 941-514-7822
Website: www.golfsmart.net
E-mail: drvarcoe@golfsmart.net

ORDERING INFORMATION

Book

Golf Smart:
7 Secrets to Master the Mind Game $19.95
Shipping & Handling   3.45

Audio Tape

For Golfers:
A Relaxation Hypnosis Program $12.95
Shipping & Handling   1.45

Please call Marilyn for information on:
Speaking / Seminars/ Coaching
Organizational Consulting